New Cari
Junior English

An Integrated Approach

HODDER EDUCATION

Orders: please contact Bookpoint Ltd, 130 Park Drive, Milton Park, Abingdon, Oxon OX14 4SE.
Telephone: (44) 01235 827720. Fax: (44) 01235 400454. Email education@bookpoint.co.uk
Lines are open from 9 a.m. to 5 p.m., Monday to Saturday, with a 24-hour message answering service.
You can also order through our website: www.hoddereducation.com

First published by Pearson Education Limited
Published from 2015 by Hodder Education,
An Hachette UK Company
Carmelite House, 50 Victoria Embankment, London EC4Y 0DZ
www.hoddereducation.com

ISBN 978 0602 25241 0

20 19 18 17 16 15
IMP 18 17 16

British Library Cataloguing in Publication Data

A full catalogue record for this book is available from the British Library.

Copyright acknowledgements

The publishers gratefully acknowledge the following for permission to reproduce copyright material:"The Origin of the Lamps" from THE SINGING TURTLE AND OTHER TALES FROM HAITI by Philipe Thoby-Marcelin and Pierre Marcelin, translated by Eva Thoby-Marcelin;'Homeless boys' taken from 'A Home for All Children' © 1980 SCM - Canterbury Press Ltd., Norwich, UK. Used by permission;'The conch shell' taken from *Encyclopedia of Jamaican Heritage* by Olive Senior, 2003, Twin Guinep Publications, Kingston, Jamaica; 'Pimento Walk' adapted from *The Young Warriors* by Vic Reid. Reproduced by permission of Pearson Education Ltd.; Book review based on the book "Harry Potter and the Philosopher's Stone" by J. K. Rowling Copyright © J. K. Rowling 1997. Every effort has been made to trace copyright holders, but if any have been inadvertently overlooked, the publishers would be happy to make the necessary arrangements at the first opportunity.

Cover design by Te Marama Design
Cover illustration by Petrina Wright
Illustrated by Geoffrey Appleton, Marlon Griffith, James Hackett, Anthony Morris, Shalini Seereeram

Printed and Bound by Hobbs the Printers, Totton, Hampshire SO40 3WX

Preface

As a result of careful examination of regional curricula, an integrated approach has been used in revising and updating materials for this fourth edition of *Caribbean Junior English*. Passages for comprehension as well as those in many exercises come from historical, scientific and cultural as well as literary sources.

Many of the original pages from the previous edition remain unchanged and new pages have been added to this edition. A chart is provided on page 119 to help teachers to use both editions in class at the same time, if necessary.

Students are given broader practice in the basic language arts skills: listening, speaking, reading and writing. The course also provides ample and varied practice in all the English topics usually taught in the junior school. Essential grammatical terms are introduced at appropriate stages, together with simple definitions, lucid explanations and challenging examples. Exercises encourage students to learn about and use reference materials - not only dictionaries and atlases, but newspapers and the wider resources of the community.

Comprehension passages have been graded according to the Flesch Reading Ease Scale to ensure that the degree of difficulty is appropriate to the age group. The scale is available at www.caribbeanschools.co.uk, together with information on readability scales, cloze procedure, methods of assessing creative writing, ideas for workshops, notes on evaluation, drills and many helpful hints on how to extend the use of this series.

Key to icons

Several icons have been added to the column on the left of the page to make this edition easy to use.

The torch is used to indicate a *Teaching point*, where a general rule is outlined and explained.

The *Word bank* defines words that the students may not be familiar with, encouraging them to keep their own bank of words and meanings.

More to do exercises at the end of each unit (a revision of *Extras* in the last edition) provide opportunities for extension work in the form of written and oral assignments. These exercises also include a variety of creative writing activities and topics for class discussion and research.

The second edition was revised and updated by Pamela Mordecai and Grace Walker Gordon. The third edition was revised by Bertilia Jean Baptiste.
Revisions for this, the fourth edition, are by Pamela Mordecai.

Contents

Nouns

Nouns are the names of people, animals, places or things.

The **dog** followed the **boy** to **school** on **Friday**.

Dog is the name of an animal.
Boy is the name of a person.
School is the name of a place.
Friday is the name of a day of the week.

A There are twenty nouns in these sentences. Find them and write them in your books.

1. It was a cool day in December.
2. Some boys were playing cricket.
3. The ball went over the fence.
4. It broke a window.
5. The glass fell in the yard.
6. It knocked some tomatoes off a bush.
7. Some birds flew into the air.
8. Dogs barked at the children.
9. A man came out with a stick in his hand.
10. Not one child was on the street.

B Write down four things you might find in each of these places.

a bedroom *bed, pillow, bedspread, mat*

1. a market
2. a farmyard
3. a kitchen
4. a school
5. a car
6. a clinic
7. an airport
8. a church
9. a bathroom
10. a garden

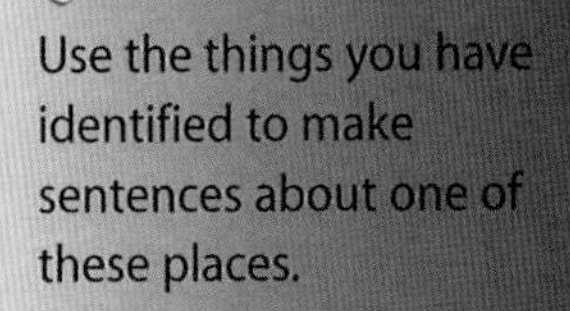

Use the things you have identified to make sentences about one of these places.

I share my bedroom with my sister. We sleep in a big double bed. We each have two pillows. There is a blue bedspread on our bed. On the floor is a big, blue and green straw mat.

Verbs

A **verb** is a word that shows action.

The children clapped their hands and danced merrily.

The words **clapped** and **danced** tell what the children did. They are verbs.

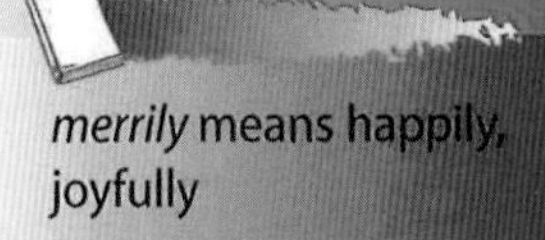

merrily means happily, joyfully

Use the three verbs you chose to write sentences about one of these persons. Read your sentences to the class.

A Find the fourteen verbs in these sentences. Write them in your books.

1. The girl walked to school.
2. She picked some flowers on the way.
3. At school, she looked for a jam jar.
4. She poured some water into the jar.
5. She carefully rested the jar with the flowers on her teacher's desk.
6. After school on Fridays, John, Ali and Joy hurry to the park.
7. They play cricket with some friends.
8. Most times, John keeps wicket while Joy bowls.
9. Ali fields and bats.
10. At five o'clock they stop and drink lemonade and chat about the game.

B Write three verbs that show an action that each of these persons might do.

a baby smile play suck

1. a shopkeeper
2. a footballer
3. a tailor
4. a gardener
5. a cricketer
6. a carpenter
7. a student
8. a pilot

Vowels

a e i o u
These letters are called vowels.
Always write **an** (not **a**) before words beginning with **a**, **e**, **i**, **o** and **u**.

an abacus is a calculator made with wire and beads
an ibis is a white or scarlet bird that lives in swampy areas
an orang-utan is a large red ape

Talk about the poem. Why do you think it is called *See what I saw, hear what I heard*? Talk about other good titles for the poem. Write your own poem using **a** and **an**. It does not have to rhyme.

- anchor
- arrow
- axe
- egg
- elephant
- ibis
- icicle
- igloo
- orange
- ostrich
- umbrella
- urn

A Write short sentences using the nouns in the list. Remember to write **an** before each.

B Write **a** or **an** in each of the spaces.

1. Henry got _a_ book for his birthday.
2. He also got _____ abacus.
3. He ate _____ ice-cream cone and _____ patty.
4. He also had _____ icicle and _____ slice of cake.
5. There was _____ ox and _____ elephant.
6. There was _____ scarlet ibis.
7. There was _____ eel.
8. And there was _____ orang-utan.
9. They were holding _____ animal council.

C Finish the poem by using **a** or **an** in the spaces below.

See what I saw, hear what I heard

I saw ____ ostrich,
_____ eel and ____ owl,
And I also heard
_____ tiger growl.

I saw ____ ibis
And ____ orang-utan
And I heard ____ bird
And ____ song that it sang.

I saw _____ elephant
And _____ egret too,
And I heard _____ rooster
Go "Cock-a-doodle-do".

Pamela Mordecai

Adjectives

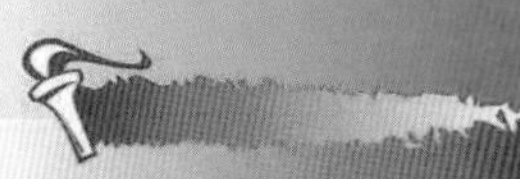

The chief of the Ashanti nation sat on a golden stool.

The word golden tells us **what kind of** stool it was.
It **describes** the noun stool, so we call it an **adjective**.
An **adjective** is a word that describes a noun.

A Copy these sentences and write out the adjectives.

1. A big car was parked in the narrow lane.
2. The rough sea battered the dark rocks.
3. Claire wore a new dress to the party.
4. The little girl was playing with a huge doll.
5. The small torch gave a brilliant light.
6. The captain of the ship had a wooden leg.
7. Tom quickly waded through the shallow river.
8. We helped the old man cross the busy road.
9. It was a steamy day.
10. We saw a clever monkey riding a tiny bicycle.

- loud
- right
- heavy
- sharp
- full
- little
- tight
- huge
- good
- angry
- leather
- beautiful

B Choose the best adjective from the list to fill each of the spaces below.

Next door there is an ________ dog.
He makes such a ________ noise.
His teeth are ________ as nails.
And he barks at ________ boys.

He has a ________ collar.
And he has a ________ chain.
His coat is ________ and black.
But his eyes are ________ of pain.

That ________ chain drags him down.
His collar is too ________ .
I think he's really a ________ dog.
Who isn't treated ________ .

Pamela Mordecai

Plurals

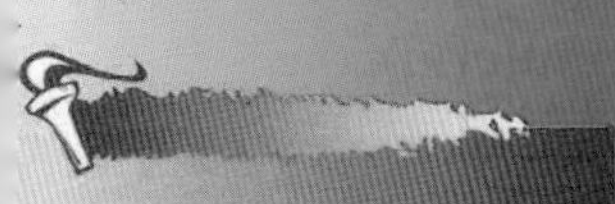

Singular means **one.**
Plural means **more than one.**

To make a noun plural, we usually add **–s** or **–es**.

Singular	Plural
boy	boy**s**
glass	glass**es**
lily	lil**ies**
leaf	lea**ves**

If a noun ends in **y**, change **y** to **i** and add **–es** to form the plural.
If a noun ends in **f**, change **f** to **v** and add **–es** to form the plural.

Divide the class into teams of eight. Each person in a team says one of the nouns in lists B, C and D, then makes it plural and spells the word. One point is given for sounding the word correctly, another point is given for the correct spelling. The team with the most points wins.

A Add **–s** to these nouns to form the plural. Use them in short sentences.

1. bird 2. cook 3. jewel 4. farmer
5. tree 6. chair 7. river 8. coat

B Add –**es** to these nouns to form the plural. Use them in short sentences.

1. bush 2. bunch 3. coach 4. brush
5. box 6. dish 7. church 8. match

C Change **y** to **i** and add **–es** to form the plural of these nouns. Use them in short sentences.

1. fly 2. country 3. baby 4. cherry
5. story 6. lady 7. party 8. penny

D Change **f** to **v** and add **–es** to form the plural of these nouns. Use them in sentences.

1. elf 2. shelf 3. loaf 4. half
5. calf 6. leaf 7. wolf 8. thief

E Copy these sentences. Make each noun in bold type plural.

1. They fed the **calf** on milk.
   They fed the calves on milk.
2. The butcher sharpened the **knife**.
3. The baker put the **loaf** on the **shelf**.
4. The gardener trimmed the **bush**.
5. The **elf** picked the **cherry**.
6. The **leaf** fell from the tree.
7. The **fly** buzzed round the **baby**.
8. The **thief** put the money in the **box**.

Comprehension: The fox and the goat

One day, a fox stopped at a well. He reached down to drink the water and with a splash, fell in. Now, the walls of the well were very high. The fox tried again and again to climb them. Alas! He could not get out.

Soon after, a goat came along. He spotted the fox in the well. Curious, he stopped. He asked the fox what he was doing there.

"I am enjoying the cool water," replied the fox. "Wouldn't you like to taste it? It is delicious."

The foolish goat did not stop to think. He just jumped down into the well. As soon as he landed on the bottom, the fox leaped onto his back. Then he scrambled quickly to the top.

The cunning fox looked down at the unhappy goat. Then he laughed. "Ah, friend goat," he warned, "next time be sure to look before you leap."

Aesop's Fables

A Finish these sentences by choosing the best answer.

1. The fox fell into the well because a) his legs were tired from his journey b) he had to stretch to get to the water c) he could not see very clearly.
2. The fox could not get out of the well because a) the walls were too high b) the walls were too slippery c) the walls were falling down.
3. The fox asked the goat to taste the water because a) he had a plan to get out of the well b) he felt sorry for the thirsty goat c) the water was really delicious.
4. The goat was unhappy because a) the water didn't taste good b) the fox had tricked him c) goats do not like cool water.
5. The story-teller calls the goat foolish because a) he didn't know the fox was a liar b) he didn't think before he acted c) he didn't mind his own business.

Verbs: forming the simple past tense

The main part of a verb is called the **root** (or **stem**). The root does not usually change when we add **–s**, **–ing** or **–ed**.

Verb	Root
cooking, cooked, cooks	cook
walking, walked, walks	walk
calling, called, calls	call

Add **–ed** to the root verb to form the simple past tense.

Verbs which add **–ed** to the root verb to form the simple past tense are **regular**.

Root verb	Simple past
touch	touch**ed**

Verbs which change the root when they form the past tense are **irregular** because they do not follow the rule.

Root verb	Simple past
eat	ate

A Write down the root verb of each of these words.

1. working
2. painting
3. calling
4. rowing
5. helps
6. clears
7. barks
8. prays
9. parked
10. crawled
11. filled
12. ended

B Fill each gap with verbs in the simple past tense by adding **–ed** to the root verb. Copy the sentences into your books.

Root verb

work 1. Yesterday, Al and Len _______ very hard.
help 2. They _______ to fix up the basic school.
pull 3. First, they _______ down all the maps and posters.
fill 4. Next, they _______ all the holes in the walls with plaster.
paint 5. Then they _______ one of the walls.
end 6. At six o'clock they _______ a long day.

C Use the simple past tense of each of these irregular verbs in the spaces in the sentences.

Root verb

come 1. My cousin Pat came to visit every Sunday.
go 2. Pat always _______ with us to church.
be 3. She _______ always ready before anyone else.
sit 4. At church, she _______ quietly during the service.
give 5. On the way home, she _______ us lots of jokes.

Verbs: adding –ed to the root verb to form the simple past tense

Verbs can tell us about actions that happened in the past (yesterday, last year).

Remember that regular verbs add **–ed** to the root verb to form the simple past tense.

A Add **–ed** to each of these verbs to form the past tense. Use the past tense verbs you have made in eight short sentences.

- hunt
- stay
- dress
- limp
- turn
- slow
- start
- climb

B To make the simple past tense (regular), add **–d** at the end of these root verbs. The **–e** is already there.

1. live
2. tinkle
3. hate
4. like
5. chase
6. scramble
7. bare
8. surprise
9. stare
10. tease

C Use the past tense verbs you have made in Exercise B to fill the gaps in this passage.

A small dog _______ beside a cat. The cat had a bell that _______ loudly. The dog _______ the noise. The cat _______ to annoy the dog with the bell. When the dog _______ it to the fence, the cat always _______ up, turned and _______ its teeth at him. One day the dog _______ the cat. The cat _______ as the nimble dog started to climb the fence. It never _______ the dog again.

Questions

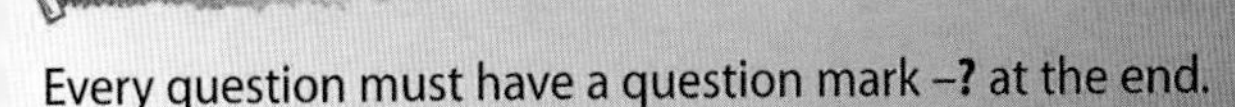

Every question must have a question mark –**?** at the end.

Is that you**?** Why were you so late**?** Where have you been**?**

There is more than one way to ask a question. Sometimes, as in the last two questions above, we use an **interrogative** (or asking) word.
Here are some interrogative words:

• who • whose • what • which • why • when • where • how

When we ask a question, we also change the position of the subject and the verb.

You were late. (Statement) Why were you late? (Question)

A Copy these questions into your books. Use the correct interrogative words from the list to fill the spaces. Put a question mark (**?**) at the end of each question. The first one is done for you.

1. Why were you absent yesterday?
2. ______ exactly did you see the doctor, in the morning or afternoon
3. ______ did you take for the fever
4. ______ are you feeling today
5. ______ told you about the party
6. ______ will they put all those people
7. ______ idea was it to rent a tent
8. ______ of these dresses should I wear to the party

B Write five sentences of your own. Use an interrogative word from the list above to begin each one.

Imagine that an aeroplane pilot is going to visit your school. Write down six questions that you would like to ask him or her.

The weather

Adjectives can be formed by adding **-y** to some words.

storm	storm**y**
cloud	cloud**y**
rain	rain**y**
wind	wind**y**
mist	mist**y**
shower	shower**y**
thunder	thunder**y**

When **-y** is added to some words, the last letter of the word is doubled.

fog	fog**gy**
sun	sun**ny**

When **-y** is added to a word ending in **-e**, this letter is dropped.

breeze breez**y**

Weather Watch

The wind, the wind
Goes whipping by.
It blows the dust
Into my eye.

The sun, the sun
Is shining down.
The glare – it makes me
Squint and frown.

The rain, the rain,
It pours and pours.
I think I'll watch
the weather from indoors.

Pamela Mordecai

A The adjectives ending with **-y** in the column on the left are used to describe the weather. Write these sentences in your books, filling each space with an adjective from the list.

Weather-Lady Sadie's Dictionary of Weather

1. Breezes whisper through the leaves on a ________ day.
2. Winds howl through the trees on a ________ day.
3. Raindrops clatter on the ground on a ________ day.
4. Showers stop and start on a ________ day.
5. The mist plays hide and seek on a ________ day.

6. The fog sits and won't move on a ________ day.
7. The thunder booms on a ________ day.
8. On a ________ day, winds, clouds, mist, rain, showers, and thunder make a terrible commotion.
9. But they all go away on a ________ day.

commotion means big fuss

B

1. Why does Sadie say that breezes whisper while winds howl?
2. Why does Sadie say that the mist plays hide and seek on a misty day?
3. What do you think of how Sadie describes a stormy day?
4. What do you think of how she describes a sunny day?
5. Sadie's dictionary is not in alphabetical order. Arrange it for her by writing the words that fill the gaps in a b c order.

Read the poem *Weather Watch* aloud several times. Why does the person in the poem want to watch the weather from indoors? Find and read the lines that tell you how the person feels about the weather. Write your own poem about the kind of weather you especially like or dislike. It does not have to rhyme.

Comprehension: The origin of the lamps

In the beginning, the sky was close to the earth. Night came and the stars shone as bright as the sun. They gave out a soft blue light. So people did not need lamps to light their homes.

There was also a very, very, tall woman. She always sat at the river's edge to wash her clothes. She was so tall that her head reached way up in the sky. It was higher than the mountains.

One morning the woman was sweeping her courtyard. The clouds decided to have some fun. They started to tease her. They tickled her neck. They pulled at her ears. The woman soon got angry.

"Come now, mischievous imps! Leave me in peace!" She scolded them crossly. The clouds burst out laughing. They teased her more than ever. They got into her ears and her nose. They twirled through her mouth and her eyes. She could not stop sneezing. She coughed and she cried. She could not help herself.

"Go away!" she finally shouted.

And she struck at them hard with her broom. The clouds drifted away. The sky was frightened too. It rose up high into space. It went far, far, up. It took all its inhabitants with it.

The sun went down that night. For the first time, people had to use lamps. The sky had gone up so far away from the earth that the stars were dim in the distance. They could no longer give light to people on earth.

Adapted from *The Singing Turtle and Other Tales from Haiti*

A Put these words from the passage into alphabetical order. Use your dictionaries to find out what they mean. Write the words and their meanings in your word bank.

- drift
- scold
- inhabitant
- dim
- mischievous
- imp

B

1. Where was the sky in the beginning?
2. How brightly did the stars shine?
3. What did the clouds do to tease the woman?
4. What did the woman do to stop the clouds from teasing her?
5. Why did the sky rise up into space?
6. Who do you think were the inhabitants of the sky?
7. Why was there no light when the sun went down?
8. What did the people have to do when the sun went down?

C Find the past tense of these root verbs in the passage. Write one sentence in which each past tense verb appears. (Some verbs appear in more than one sentence.) Underline the verb in the past tense. The first one is done for you. If you need help, use your dictionary.

1. be — In the beginning, the sky was close to the earth.
2. come
3. give
4. do
5. sit
6. get
7. strike
8. rise

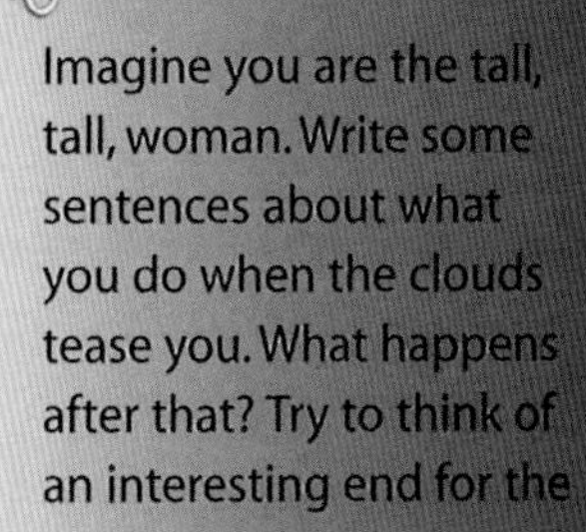

Verbs: adding –ing to form the present continuous tense

We can form the present tense in more than one way.

Simple present tense	Present continuous tense
He dances.	He is dancing.

The present continuous tense says that the action is still going on or continuing.
To form the present continuous tense we add **–ing** to the root verb and we use **am, is** and **are** as helping words.

Present	Present continuous
I dance	I **am** danc**ing**
you dance	you **are** danc**ing**
he, she, it dances	he, she, it **is** danc**ing**
we dance	we **are** danc**ing**
you dance	you **are** danc**ing**
they dance	they **are** danc**ing**

A Change each sentence in the present tense to the present continuous. The first one is done for you.

	Present tense	**Present continuous tense**
1.	Clem gets up.	Clem is getting up.
2.	He dresses.	
3.	He goes downstairs.	
4.	He eats his breakfast.	
5.	He rushes outside.	
6.	He waves down the school bus.	
7.	He jumps in.	

B Change the verbs in this passage from the present continuous tense to the present tense.

The rain is falling heavily. It is stinging Chitra's face. She is running. Her legs are hurting. Her head is aching. Her eyes are filling with tears. Suddenly she is standing in front of the house. Grandma Ali is waiting at the window. She is opening the door. She is hugging Chitra.

Rhymes

- gown
- down
- bringing
- singing
- brother
- mother
- bells
- tells
- drum
- come
- trees
- breeze

Talk about the word **holiday**. Where does it come from? Talk about the things in your town or country that tell that Christmas, Easter, Passover, Divali, Hosay or any other holiday is coming.

Write your own poem about a holiday. Use adjectives and verbs that make you see, hear, taste and smell what is happening.

A Copy the poem filling in the missing rhymes which are in the list on the left.

Caribbean Carol

Here we have no jingle bells
here the poinsettia ______
with the white Euphorbia ______
and the gentlest Christmas ______
that the Son of God is born.

Here the bamboo fife and drum
play the tune that Christ is ______.
Sun as bright as angels ______
news to shepherds with their ______,
skies as blue as Mary's ______
say that Jesus has come ______
as a baby, our ______,
with a simple, human ______.

Pamela Mordecai

B

1. What three things in the Caribbean say that the Son of God is born? Read the lines that tell you.
2. What musical instruments are used to play the tune that Christ has come? Read the line that tells you.
3. What is the Caribbean sun as bright as?
4. What are the skies as blue as?
5. What do the sun and skies say?

C Talk about how to read the poem. Think about which lines are joyful, and therefore strong, and which lines should be should be soft and gentle. Then read the poem all together.

Verbs: the present continuous

To form the present continuous tense we add **-ing** to the root verb and we use **am**, **is** and **are** as helping words.

When it is used with a helping word to form a tense, we call the **-ing** word a present participle.

When there is a vowel (**a**, **e**, **i**, **o**, **u**) before the final **-e** we add **-ing** to the root verb.

see seeing

When there is a consonant before the final **-e** we drop the **-e** and add **-ing** to the root verb.

serve serving

A Write **–ing** after each root verb. Drop the **–e** at the end. Then use the words you have made to form the present continuous tense. Put them in the sentences. The first one is done for you.

1. blaze — The fire is blazing through the field of dry grass.
2. dance — The sailors are _______ a jig.
3. sneeze — I am _______ because I ate too much pepper.
4. move — He is _______ to a school in San Fernando.
5. share — Is he _______ his chocolates with the rest of you?
6. tease — If you are _______ your sister again, I'll send you to bed.
7. leave — My grandfather is _______ on the first plane.
8. hope — We are _______ to come first in the quiz competition.
9. take — They are _______ a long time to get here.

B Sam is at scout camp. This is a letter he is writing to his parents. Because he is telling them about the things that are going on when he is writing, he is using the present continuous tense. Add **–ing** to the root verbs to form the present continuous tense.

Dear Mum and Dad,

The mosquitoes are (**bite**) already, even though the sun is just (**rise**) . I am (**race**) to get dressed. The delicious smell from the kitchen is (**make**) my mouth water. It's as if, right this very minute, I am (**taste**) the cornbread and eggs and bacon. Also, the scoutmaster is (**give**) out insect spray this morning, and I need some. He told us that he is not (**save**) any for those who are (**snore**). The boys with the worst bites are already (**soothe**) their itches by bathing in the salt seawater. I am going to swim too, but right now, I am (**dive**) into breakfast. Get it? Ha ha!

Much love,
Your son,

Sam

Dictionary work

If two words begin with the same letter, like hand and head, we look at the second letter to put them in alphabetical order. The letter **a** comes before the letter **e** in the alphabet, so hand comes before head.

A Look at the first letter of each word in the two lists below. Write each group of words in alphabetical order.

1. head
train
before
food
also

2. look
ready
wind
another
small

B Put these words in correct alphabetical order. Use your dictionaries to find out what they mean. Then write them into your word bank.

3. stumble
slide
survive
smartest
sited

C Use the words from List 3 in sentences 1–5 below. The words are used in alphabetical order in the sentences. Write the sentences in your books.

1. The telephone box was _______ on the road at the bottom of the slope.
2. Tom didn't want to _______ down the steep hillside.
3. But he knew it was the _______ and safest way to get down.
4. He was worried when he saw the old man _______ and hit his head.
5. He knew the man would not _______ if he did not get to a phone quickly.

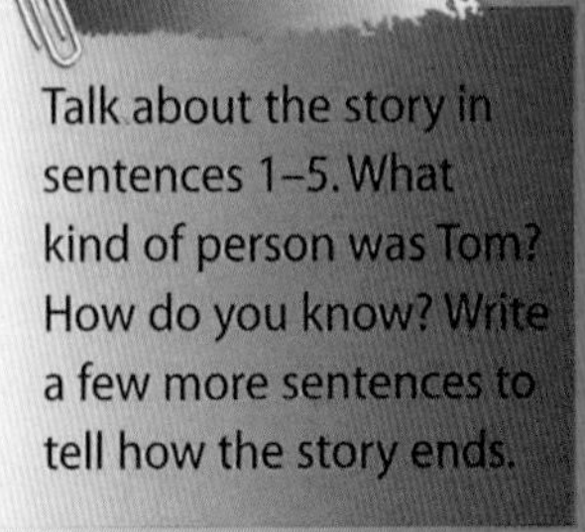

Talk about the story in sentences 1–5. What kind of person was Tom? How do you know? Write a few more sentences to tell how the story ends.

Verbs: using is/are, was/were

Singular	Plural	Singular	Plural
is	**are**	**was**	**were**
This apple **is** juicy.	These apples **are** juicy.	The boy **was** sad.	The boys **were** sad.
We use **is** for **one** apple.	We use **are** for **more than one** apple.	We use **was** for **one** boy.	We use **were** for **more than one** boy.

A Choose the right word from the pair above to fill each space.

1. is are
   Two men ______ holding one end of the rope.
2. is are
   One man ______ holding the other end.
3. was were
   Several cows ______ grazing in the field.
4. was were
   The boy ______ afraid of the bull.

B Use the right word from the pair in bold type to complete each sentence.

Errol Henry's mother (**is/are**) up early. She (**is/are**) at the table in the kitchen. On the table (**is/are**) loaves of bread and all kinds of things for making sandwiches. Mangoes, oranges and bananas (**is/are**) in a basket on the ground. The Henrys (**is/are**) going for a picnic. Mrs. Henry (**is/are**) making final preparations. Yesterday they (**was/were**) in town all morning. Mrs. Henry (**was/were**) in the supermarket buying groceries. Errol and Lydia (**was/were**) in the market getting fruit. Mr. Henry (**was/were**) at the gas station filling up the car with gas.

Talk about the passage. What preparations did the Henrys make? What preparations do you make when you go on a picnic? Do you like picnics? Write some sentences explaining why you do or do not like going on picnics.

Comprehension: Pitch

Winston woke up early. He was going to work with his father. They were going to a site in Bridgetown. Mr. Shephard drove a steamroller at the site. It was one of the big ones that levelled the roads.

"Daddy, how do they make asphalt?" Winston asked his father.

"Asphalt is made from pitch, son," Mr. Shephard replied. "Pitch is found in the earth. It is a dark brown or black substance. When it is cool, it is hard. When it is heated, it becomes liquid, so it can be poured. The pitch or tar is mixed with sand and stones. That is how we make the asphalt that we use to pave the roads."

"Can we find pitch if we dig in our backyard, Daddy?"

"I don't think so son. But if you visit Trinidad you will find as much pitch as you can use. Most of the pitch in the world comes from the famous Pitch Lake. It's an odd lake. It's mostly solid. Here and there on the top are little puddles of water. When you dig out a block of pitch, the rest of the pitch in the lake just fills it up again." His father smiled.

"How big is it?" asked Winston.

"It covers about forty hectares. And it is about thirty metres deep. One of these days we'll visit Trinidad. Then you can see for yourself."

A Find these words in the passage. Then choose the meaning that matches the way the word is used.

1. Site means

   a) scenery b) affair c) place.

2. Levelled means
   a) patted b) equalled c) flattened.
3. Pitch means
   a) asphalt b) tar c) stones.
4. Substance means
   a) material b) ground c) underground.
5. Pave means
   a) cover b) dig c) level.
6. Odd means
   a) humorous b) ordinary c) strange.

B

1. Winston's father was
   a) the boss at a work site in Bridgetown
   b) the driver of a big steamroller
   c) the person who got pitch from Trinidad.
2. Pitch or tar is found
   a) in the sea
   b) in water
   c) in the earth.
3. When pitch is cool, it is
   a) liquid
   b) sandy
   c) solid.
4. When it is hot, pitch can be
   a) poured
   b) cut up in blocks
   c) sliced like cheese.
5. Most of the world's pitch comes from
   a) Barbados
   b) Trinidad
   c) England.

Write three sentences about the Pitch Lake or write three sentences explaining how asphalt is made.

C Talk about why the Pitch Lake is called a lake.

Using capital letters

Capital letters are used:
- to begin a sentence;
- for the names of people and pets;
- for Mr., Mrs., Dr.;
- for the names of places such as islands, rivers, mountains, towns, regions;
- for addresses;
- for the names of the days of the week;
- for the word **I**.

A Copy these sentences, using capital letters where they are needed.

1. henry martin lives in kingstown.
2. the world's best arrowroot is grown in st. vincent.
3. david and I are going to barbados for the holidays.
4. we hope to go next friday.
5. the highest mountains in jamaica are the blue mountains.
6. castries is the capital of st. lucia.
7. a new shop has just opened on king street.
8. dr. mais is my doctor and dr. lawrence is my dentist.
9. colin has a parrot named pepper.
10. we paid a visit to mr. and mrs. lowe.

Words with more than one meaning (1)

Some words have more than one meaning.

The brown **bear** climbed the tree.
Sandra could hardly **bear** the pain.

- bark
- light
- blow
- match
- chest
- ring
- fair
- can
- kind
- watch

A Use the words from the list on the left to fill the spaces in the sentences. The same word must be used for each pair of sentences.

1. I bought a _______ of fruit juice.
   Myrna _______ read well.
2. The _______ woman gave $100 to the library fund.
   This is a different _______ of football.
3. It is time to _______ the school bell.
   The wedding _______ was made of solid gold.
4. The mango tree has a rough _______.
   The dog began to _______ when the children teased him.
5. Much damage is done when high winds _______.
   A _______ on the head knocked the boxer out.
6. The weatherman said it would be _______ today.
   There were many amusements at the _______.
7. My new _______ keeps very good time.
   We did not _______ television last night.
8. The parcel was as _______ as a feather.
   Scouts learn to _______ a fire by rubbing sticks together.
9. There was a big crowd at the football _______.
   Grandpa struck a _______ and lit his pipe.
10. James has a cold on his _______.
    The treasure was hidden in an iron _______.

Get into groups of three or four. Write down as many words you can think of that have more than one meaning. Your teacher will tell you how much time you have. The group with the most words wins.

Developing dialogue

Brothers and sisters sometimes have disagreements. Here is an argument between two sisters, Lisa and Desi.

LISA Desi, I don't want you wearing my socks to school.

DESI But Lisa, my socks were wet so I had to borrow yours.

LISA I don't care about your wet socks, just don't use my things.

DESI You use my things too, and I never make a fuss.

LISA

DESI

LISA

DESI

A Talk about the argument. Do you think Lisa is right? Do you agree with Desi? Write the rest of the conversation, showing how it ended.

B Here are some examples of things that cause disagreements.

- Cheating at games
- Not doing chores
- Not taking care of things that are borrowed

Make a list of things that cause you and your brother or sister or friend to disagree. Choose one thing from your list and write what you both say when you argue about this matter. Set out the conversation in the same way that Desi and Lisa's argument is set out. Use your name and the name of the person you are fussing with.

Homophones (1)

Here and **hear** sound alike but we spell them differently.

There and **their** sound alike but we spell them differently.

Words that sound alike but are spelled differently are called **homophones**.

Here means in this place.
I left the bag here five minutes ago.

Hear is what you do with your ears.
We could hear the birds singing.

There means in that place.
He lives over there.

Their means belonging to them.
The boys played with their football.

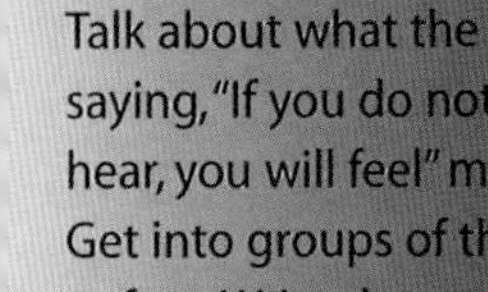

Talk about what the saying, "If you do not hear, you will feel" means. Get into groups of three or four. Write down as many words you can think of that sound alike but are spelt differently. The group with the most words wins.

A Write **here** or **hear** in each space.

1. Will you stay ______ until I come back?
2. Ann did not ______ her mother calling her.
3. We could ______ someone snoring in the next room.
4. ______is the ball you were looking for.
5. Would you like to live ______?
6. My dad says, "If you do not ______ , you will feel."

B Write **there** or **their** in each space.

1. The children gave ______ dog a bath.
2. I waited ______ for nearly an hour.
3. The cricket balls are in the bag over ______ .
4. Have they found ______ cricket pads?
5. The two boys went to the movie with ______ cousin.
6. I saw patches of weeds here and ______ on the lawn.

Comprehension: Anansi and Snake

Anansi set the long piece of bamboo on the ground beside Snake. He wanted to see which was longer. Then he said:

"But Snake, this cannot work. When I go up to see where your head is, you crawl up. When I go down to see where your tail is, you crawl down. That way you will always seem to be longer than the bamboo pole."

"Tie my tail, then!" said Snake. "Tie my tail! I know that I am longer than the bamboo, never mind what you say."

Anansi tied Snake's tail to one end of the bamboo pole. Then he ran up to the other end.

"Stretch, Snake, stretch! Stretch and we will see who is longer." A crowd of animals was gathering round.

Snake stretched as hard as he could. Anansi tied him round his middle.

"That's so you won't slip back," he said to Snake. Then Anansi ran back up to his head.

"Rest yourself for a little, Snake. Now stretch again. Ten centimetres more and you will be longer than the piece of bamboo. Try your hardest. Stretch so that you have to shut your eyes tight."

Snake made a mighty effort. He stretched hard. He stretched till he had to squeeze his eyes shut.

"Hooray!" cried the animals, "You are winning, Snake. Just four centimetres more."

And at that moment Anansi tied Snake's head to the bamboo pole. The animals fell silent. Yes, there was Snake all tied up. And feeble Anansi had caught him all by himself.

Adapted from *Anansi the Spider Man* by Philip Sherlock.

A Write down the words in List A. Write next to each, the word or phrase from List B which could replace it in the passage without changing the meaning.

A	B
squeeze	try
mighty	weak
effort	became
moment	great
fell	press together
feeble	exact time

B

1. Did Anansi have more than one reason for putting the bamboo beside Snake? Explain.
2. Why did Anansi ask Snake to rest?
3. Why were the animals cheering?
4. Why do you think the animals fell silent?
5. Why did Anansi want to trick Snake?
6. What do you think of Anansi? What do you think of Snake?
7. Think of a better title for the story. Explain why it is better.

C Now that Anansi has Snake tied up, what do you think is going to happen? Do you think Snake is worried? Do you think Anansi is going to let Snake go? Work in groups of three or four. Make up a conversation between Anansi and Snake that tells what happens next. Begin like this:

SNAKE Brer Anansi, you can't keep me tied up to this bamboo pole.

ANANSI

SNAKE

ANANSI

SNAKE

Read the conversations to the class. Different pairs of students can take turns reading the parts of Anansi and Snake.

Full stops, commas

We put a full stop at the end of every sentence that makes a statement.

The hurricane ruined all the crops**.**

We put a question mark at the end of every sentence that asks a question.

Did the hurricane ruin all the crops**?**

When the names of three or four things come together, we separate them by using commas **(,)** .

For lunch we had fish**,** rice**,** greens and juice**.**

Notice that there is no comma between the last two things. This is because the word **and** separates them.

A Copy each sentence. Put a full stop or a question mark at the end of each.

1. The flying fish has two large fins
2. Dolphins are very clever creatures
3. Have you visited the Caroni Swamp
4. Sharks can eat people
5. Will you call for me in the morning
6. Our school starts at nine o'clock
7. Did you post the letter I gave you
8. Can an anaconda snake swallow a whole cow

B Copy these sentences. Put in the commas.

1. Robert Elaine Carol Michael and Peter were ill.
2. The fishermen caught lobsters shrimp crab and kingfish.
3. Kingston Port of Spain Bridgetown and Belize are all cities.
4. The colours of the rainbow are red orange yellow green blue indigo and violet.
5. At the zoo we saw a lion a tiger a tapir and several monkeys.

Forming nouns

Some nouns are formed by adding **–ness** to words.

sad	sadness
slow	slowness
deaf	deafness
stout	stoutness

When **–ness** is added to words ending with **–y**, the **y** is changed to **i**.

friendly	friendl**iness**
shabby	shabb**iness**
sleepy	sleep**iness**

A Add **–ness** to these adjectives. Use them to fill the gaps.

1. **glad** My heart filled with _____ when I got home.
2. **quick** I was amazed by the _____ of his feet.
3. **tired** Overcome by _____ , Al fell asleep.
4. **loud** She hated the _____ of the thunder.
5. **sore** I took a pill for the _____ in my throat.
6. **blind** Jesus cured the man of his _____ .
7. **rough** The _____ of the sea alarmed Leo.
8. **fresh** I love the _____ of the morning air.

B Form nouns from the adjectives in bold type. Use them to fill the gaps.

1. The new girl thanked Jo for her ________. (**friendly**)
2. Sue smiled at the ________ of the rabbits. (**jumpy**)
3. Holidays usually bring much ________ . (**happy**)
4. The ________ of the roads is quite usual early in the morning. (**empty**)
5. The groom gasped at the ________ of the bride. (**lovely**)
6. The old man suffered from ________. (**giddy**)
7. The boys were delighted by the ________ of the plane ride. (**bumpy**)
8. The duckling grew up and left her ________ behind. (**ugly**)
9. The teacher scolded Kaye for her ________ . (**lazy**)
10. Stan slept badly because of the ________ of the mattress. (**lumpy**)

Verbs: doubling consonants before adding –ed and –ing

When we add **–ed** or **–ing** to each of the words in this list we double the last letter.

nod
nod**ded**
nod**ding**

hum
hum**med**
hum**ming**

drop
drop**ped**
drop**ping**

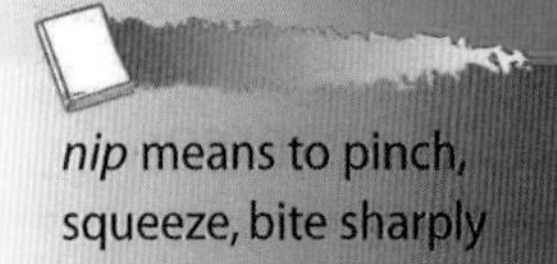

nip means to pinch, squeeze, bite sharply

A Add **–ing** to each root verb. Double the last letter.

1. hop
2. chat
3. rob
4. clap
5. hum
6. skim
7. drum
8. skid
9. drag
10. slip

B Add **–ed** to each root verb. Double the last letter.

1. snap
2. grin
3. lap
4. rub
5. nip
6. dip
7. trim
8. grab
9. slam
10. drip

C Fill each space with the right root verb from the lists above. Add **–ing** or **–ed** as needed.

1. Water was ______ from a hole in the can.
2. The truck ______ on the wet road.
3. Joy ______ a tune as she worked.
4. The fierce dog ______ at the small boy.
5. The boat ______ and rose on the waves.
6. The rude boy ______ the door as he left.
7. Jo ______ on a mango skin and hurt her leg.
8. The gardener was busy ______ the hedge.
9. A lovely black kitten was ______ up a saucer of milk.
10. The little rabbits ______ about in the yard.

Verbs: adding –es and –ed

When **–es** or **–ed** is added to a verb ending with **–y**, this letter is first changed to **i**.

I try hard.
He tr**ies** hard.
She tr**ied** hard.

A Fill the gaps by changing the **–y** at the end of the verb to **i** and adding **–es**.

1. Lily ______ hard at school. (**try**)
2. She never ______ through her work. (**hurry**)
3. The baby always ______ his bottle. (**empty**)
4. Then he ______ for more. (**cry**)
5. Sam ______ his baby sister across the muddy road. (**carry**)
6. He ______ his clothes but his sister stays clean. (**dirty**)

B Fill the gaps by changing the **–y** at end of the verb to **i** and adding **–ed**.

1. Tim ______ fish and chips every Friday. (**fry**)
2. He ______ the kitchen every time. (**dirty**)
3. He had to clean up every spot that his Mum ______ . (**spy**)
4. The old scribe ______ the prince's words every morning. (**copy**)
5. As soon as the ink ______ on the pages, he put them in a magic basket. (**dry**)
6. Then he ______ the basket to the king. (**carry**)

C Finish each sentence by using the right form of the verb in bold type. Add **–es** or **–ed** as needed.

1. Paul ______ eggs for breakfast. (**fry**)
2. Sita ______ her best dress with mud. (**dirty**)
3. She ______ because she cut her knee. (**cry**)
4. We ______ but we missed the bus. (**hurry**)
5. The hungry cat ______ to grab the rat. (**try**)

scribe means a person who, long ago, used to copy books by hand. It also means a writer or a secretary.

Verbs: did/has done/have done; went/has gone/have gone

Do, **go** and **see** are irregular verbs.
They are irregular because they do not add **-ed** to show the past tense. Instead, they change the form of the root verb.

To show the past time of **do** we use **did**.

He **did** his work well.

We can also use **has done** and **have done** for past time.
The word **done** always needs a helping word.

He **has done** his work. (helping word: has)
They **have done** the job. (helping word: have)

To show the past time of **go** we use **went**.

They **went** to the beach.

We can also use **has gone** and **have gone** for past time.
The word **gone** always needs a helping word.

A Use the correct word to finish each sentence.

1. Ann (**did/done**) her best to tidy the garage.
2. The boys have (**went/gone**)to the cricket field.
3. It is the best drawing I have (**did/done**).
4. Chitra's parents (**went/gone**) to get diyas for the Divali festival.
5. Colin has (**did/done**) many sketches of his sisters and brothers.
6. Have you children (**did/done**) your chores?
7. She (**went/gone**) to the hospital to see her new baby sister.
8. I have (**went/gone**) to church with my parents since I was a baby.

More irregular past tenses

We do not always add **–ed** to verbs to show the past time.
Some verbs such as **be**, **do**, **go** and **saw**, change their shape to show past time.

	Simple present tense	Simple past tense
be	Today **I am** happy.	Yesterday **I was** happy.
do	Today **I do** my homework.	Yesterday **I did** my homework.
go	Today **I go** to dancing class.	Yesterday **I went** to dancing class.
see	Today **I see** the doctor.	Yesterday **I saw** the doctor.

These verbs change the root to show the simple past tense.

Root verb	Simple past tense
begin	began
do	did
feel	felt
eat	ate
find	found
go	went
know	knew
meet	met
ring	rang
rise	rose
run	ran
see	saw
stand	stood
take	took
think	thought
wear	wore

A Choose past tense verbs from the list on the left. Put them in the right gaps in the passage.

That day Alma ______ a black dress for the very first time. She ______ for many minutes outside the principal's office. She ______ very sad and confused. But she finally ______ in. The principal, Mrs. Bell, ______ from her chair to greet her. She ______ to speak first. "Oh, Alma. You ______ that we ______ about your Mum. But we ______ not. We only ______ out this morning. Your aunt ______ to say that she ______ you as you were leaving school, and ______ you to the hospital right away."

B Change the verbs from the present to the simple past tense.

I hardly eat any breakfast, and now, I stand in the line, scared. I wear my brain out with worry. Every now and then I rise on my toes, trying to see up to the front. Soon I go inside and I begin the Spanish test. I think of all the words. I take my time. I run them all slowly through my mind. And I know them all – every single one!

Comprehension: Homeless boys

Barnardo was startled by what he heard. Could it be true that this ten-year-old boy really had no parents and no home?

"Are there other boys like you, Jim, without a home?" asked Barnardo.

"Oh, yes, lots of 'em," was the reply.

Surely the boy must be telling a lie, thought Barnardo. But suppose he was telling the truth.

"I will give you a meal and a bed for the night, Jim. Will you show me where these boys sleep?"

Jim jumped at the chance. He had never slept in a proper bed. And so at 12.30 a.m. the two of them set out. They walked the streets looking for sleeping children. At first there was no sign of anybody sleeping out. Barnardo was beginning to think that Jim must have made it all up. Then Jim led the way down a side passage. It ended in a high wall. Beyond it was the roof of an old clothes shop.

"They're up there," explained Jim. He pointed to the roof. He climbed the wall. Then he pulled his teacher up behind him. And there on the flat part of the roof lay eleven poorly dressed boys – fast asleep. They were huddled close together to keep themselves warm. Their ages were from about eight to eighteen years.

The Story of Dr Barnardo by Geoffrey Hanks

A Find these words in the passage. Then choose the meaning that matches the way the word is used.

1. Startled means
   a) amused b) surprised c) excited.
2. Reply means
   a) answer b) talk c) question.
3. Proper means
   a) sturdy b) real c) tidy.
4. Passage means
   a) narrow walkway b) fares c) travel.
5. Beyond means
   a) on top of b) in the distance
   c) on the far side of.
6. Huddled means
   a) crowded b) stooped c) shivering.

B Read the passage. Answer these questions in complete sentences in your books.

1. Why was Barnardo startled?
2. Did Jim have a home? Explain.
3. Why did Barnardo think that Jim was not telling the truth?
4. Barnardo tells Jim he will give him a bed. Then he asks Jim to show him where the boys are. Do you think this was fair? Explain.
5. Where did they find the boys?
6. Why do you think the boys slept on a high roof?
7. How did they keep themselves warm?
8. What did Jim do for the first time in his life that night?

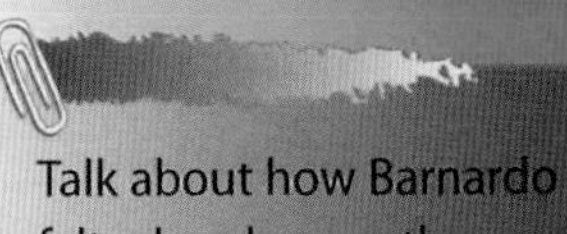

Talk about how Barnardo felt when he saw the boys. Did his opinion of Jim change? Why do you think these boys were homeless? Imagine that you had to leave home. Write some sentences about the things you would miss most.

Adjectives: formed by adding –y to nouns

We learned on page 10 that adjectives can be formed by adding **–y** to some words.

rust	rust**y**
greed	greed**y**
salt	salt**y**
wealth	wealth**y**
wind	wind**y**

When **–y** is added to some words the last letter of the word is doubled.

sun	su**nny**
fog	fo**ggy**
skin	ski**nny**
fur	fu**rry**
bag	ba**ggy**

When **–y** is added to a word ending with **e** this letter is dropped.

noise	nois**y**
smoke	smok**y**
ease	eas**y**
shade	shad**y**
stone	ston**y**

A Replace the words in bold type with adjectives formed by adding **–y** to the noun.

1. We spent Sunday at Princess Beach, which is **covered with sand**.
2. It was a day **of strong winds**.
3. The sea was blue and **full of salt**.
4. It was beautiful and **covered with foam**.
5. In the morning the sky was **full of clouds**.
6. But the sun came out and it became bright and **full of glitter**.
7. Above the beach is a hill **with many rocks**.
8. The top of the mountain is like a flat table **covered with dust**.
9. We climbed up and when we got to the top, we were **covered with dirt**.
10. When we looked out at the view we all felt **that we had lots of luck**.

B What are the missing adjectives?

1. It was a ________ day. (**sun**)
2. Karin sat in an ________ chair. (**ease**)
3. The chair was under a ________ tree. (**shade**)
4. The tree was beside a ________ path. (**stone**)
5. Beside her was her ________ cat. (**fur**)
6. She patted it with a ________ hand. (**skin**)
7. Since she had been ill, her dress was ________. (**bag**)
8. She loved the chatter of the ________ birds. (**noise**)

Subject and verb

Every sentence contains a subject and a verb. The verb tells the action. To find the subject ask "Who or what?" before the verb.

The wind howled

What is the verb? Howled.
Who or what howled? The wind.
The noun **wind** is the subject of the verb **howled**.

A In each of these sentences, the verb is underlined. Make three columns in your books. Call them Sentence, Question and Subject. Write out each sentence then ask the question "Who or what?" before the verb. The answer you get is the subject. Write the subject in the last column. The first one is done for you.

	Sentence	Question	Subject
1.	The thunder rolled.	What rolled?	The thunder
2.	The lightening flashed.	What flashed?	
3.	The rain poured.	What poured?	
4.	The children shivered.	Who shivered?	
5.	The old man entered.	Who entered?	
6.	The old lady followed.	Who followed?	
7.	The children looked up.	Who looked?	
8.	The lady gave them blankets.	Who gave?	
9.	Everybody slept soundly.	Who slept?	

Play a game. Everyone sits in a circle. The first person gives a noun to be the subject of a sentence. Then the next person finishes the sentence by adding the verb. For example, Person One: "Subject: The birds." Person two: "Sentence: The birds ate the crumbs." Continue around the circle. Let every one have a turn.

B Match each subject with the right verb. Then write out the sentences.

	Subject	Verb
1.	The sun	peck greedily.
2.	The cock	buzz busily.
3.	The flowers	begins.
4.	The bees	rises.
5.	The birds	open softly.
6.	A new day	crows loudly.

Joining sentences using so

We often use the words **and** and **but** to join sentences.
We can also use the word **so**.

The sea became rough.
Mum said we should stay on the beach.

The sea became rough **so** Mum said we should stay on the beach.

It started to rain.
We went home.

It started to rain **so** we went home.

A Join each pair of sentences using the word **so**.

1. It was a fine day.
   We climbed Shelter Mountain.
2. Paul had lost his bus fare.
   He had to walk home.
3. The old man was tired.
   He sat down to rest.
4. The children had mumps.
   They could not go to school.
5. Bill had no money.
   He could not buy an ice-cream cone.
6. Prakesh felt hot.
   He took his shirt off.
7. The weather was wet.
   We wore our raincoats.
8. The garden gate was open.
   The goats came in and ate the vegetables.

Homophones (2)

On page 25 you learned that words that sound alike but are spelled differently are called **homophones**. Look at these four pairs of words.

bare A **bare** tree has no leaves.

bear The polar **bear** is a very big animal.

dear The dress was too **dear** so she did not buy it.
Jane is a very **dear** friend of mine.

deer A **deer** is a graceful animal.

road The **road** runs from Kingston to Spanish Town.

rode Mary **rode** a donkey to Bethlehem.

heel The back part of your foot is called the **heel**.

heal To **heal** a person means to make him well.

A Choose the correct word from the pair below to complete each sentence.

1. Sandra began her letter, "My ______ Mum". (**dear/deer**)
2. The cut on your finger will soon ______ . (**heel/heal**)
3. Mother Hubbard's cupboard was ______ . (**bear/bare**)
4. The ______ of the woman's shoe came right off. (**heel/heal**)
5. They are building a new ______ . (**rode/road**)
6. The koala ______ is found in Australia. (**bear/bare**)
7. The book had a ______ , a lion and a giraffe on the cover. (**dear/deer**)
8. The boys ______ into town. (**rode/road**)

B Choose the correct word from each pair in the following passage.

"That (**road/rode**) is bumpy," Pam's mother said. "And every now and then a (**dear/deer**) runs across suddenly. So be careful." Pam set off. She (**road/rode**) her bike slowly. She was thinking of the (**bear/bare**) she saw at the circus. It had on a skirt and hat, and looked like a (**dear/deer**) little old lady. Suddenly the bike hit a rock and fell over. The (**heal/heel**) of one of Pam's shoes broke off and she had cuts on both legs. Her legs were (**bear/bare**) since she was wearing shorts. Some of the cuts were bad. "They will take a long time to (**heal/heel**)," she thought, as she struggled to get up.

Similar words

a wealthy man
a rich man

The words **wealthy** and **rich** have much the same meaning.

Learn the list of similar words.

assist	help
difficult	hard
complete	finish
wicked	bad
commence	begin
hasten	hurry
peril	danger
naked	bare
seize	grab
courageous	brave

A Replace each word in bold type with a simpler word.

1. The concert will **commence** at 7 o'clock.
2. Hubert found the sum very **difficult**.
3. The ship was in great **peril**.
4. The **wicked** fairy cast a spell over the prince.
5. The **courageous** sailor saved the boy's life.
6. "It's your Pa, boy," the giant roared. "**Hasten** to the door."
7. He **seized** the lifeguard's rope just in time.
8. The sun shone on the swimmer's **naked** back.
9. "Will you **assist** me, sir?" the lady asked.
10. He **completed** the race in record time.

B From each group below select the word that is similar in meaning to the one in bold type.

1. **seize**	2. **hasten**	3. **peril**	4. **assist**
hit	fix	fear	help
tear	hurry	ruin	coax
twist	work	danger	hinder
grab	play	end	wait

5. **difficult**	6. **commence**	7. **courageous**
clever	praise	silly
easy	change	brave
hard	begin	short
simple	correct	noisy

8. **naked**	9. **complete**	10. **wicked**
empty	fix	cunning
dressed	finish	good
poor	work	bad
bare	begin	tricky

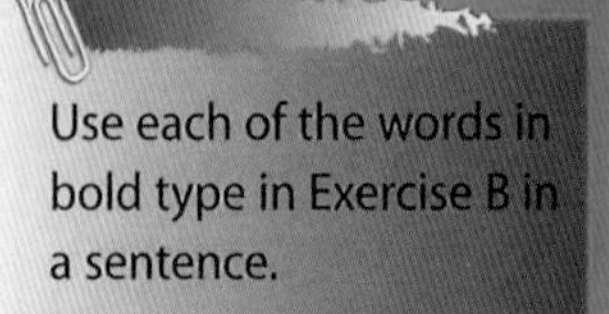

Use each of the words in bold type in Exercise B in a sentence.

Using the apostrophe to show ownership

I like Simon**'s** new puppy.

The **'s** in Simon's shows that the puppy **belongs to** Simon.
It is his. He owns it.
We call this ' mark an **apostrophe**.
It is used to show ownership and is usually followed by **s**.

Long way
- the kite belonging to Paul
- the wool of the sheep

Short way (using the apostrophe)
- Paul's kite
- the sheep's wool

A Copy these into your books, putting in the ' before the **s**.

1. the elephant s trunk
2. the sailor s cap
3. the horse s mane
4. the rabbit s tail
5. the old man s beard
6. the cat s paws
7. the hen s egg
8. the spider s web
9. the pig s snout
10. the lion s mane

B Copy these sentences using the apostrophe.

1. Here is **the book belonging to Mary**.
2. There is **the bat which belongs to Peter**.
3. Where is **the ribbon belonging to Ann**?
4. How fast is **the watch that belongs to Father**?
5. I found **the ring that belongs to Mother**.

C Copy these sentences using the apostrophe. The first one is done for you.

1. When the prince touched his arm, he felt **the fur of a cat**.
   When the prince touched his arm, he felt a cat's fur.
2. When he touched his mouth, he felt **the beak of a parrot**.
3. Instead of his own ears, he felt **the ears of a donkey**.
4. And out from the side of his head grew **the horns of a cow**.
5. He knew then that he should not have touched **the magic nest of the swan**.

Comprehension: The conch shell

The conch shell is a lovely, big, pink shell. It is perhaps the best-known shell in the Caribbean.

The conch is a shellfish. The shell is its home. The first occupants of the northern Caribbean were Ciboneys. They found the conch very useful. They ate its flesh. They used the shell to make crude axes. They used it to make simple tools. They used it for cups and other vessels. They even used it to make music.

The Tainos came after the Ciboneys. They also ate conch flesh. And they too used the shell for many things. They made tools. They made containers. They made jewellery. They carved images of their zemis from it. Zemis were their spirits. The Tainos made trumpets from conch shells. Warriors blowing these trumpets led them into battle. They also carved a horn from it. It was called the fotuto. They used it in special rites.

In later times Caribbean people continued to use the shell to keep in contact. In many islands it was sounded to summon people. This was useful in times of danger. Vendors used it to tell their customers they were passing by. It was used to wake workers. It told them when to start work. It told them when to stop. It went on serving this purpose up until the twentieth century.

A Find these words in the passage. Then choose the meaning that matches the way the word is used.

1. Occupants means a) houses b) people who live (in a place) c) conquerors.
2. Crude means a) rough b) unmannerly c) oily.
3. Vessels means a) ships b) vases c) containers.
4. Images means a) paintings b) photographs c) statues.
5. Battle means a) force b) army c) war.
6. Rites means a) ceremonies b) goodness c) truths.
7. In contact means a) in exchange b) in touch c) in relation.
8. Summon means a) pastor's talk at a church service b) call together c) shout at.

Imagine you are a conch and that you live in a beautiful shell. Think of what your surroundings under the water or on the shore look like, of the other creatures that live in the sea with you, of the noises you hear, of the things you feel (cold, warm) and touch (sand, waves, rocks). Write a poem about your life, or about anything special in it, for example, the danger when people try to catch you. Use words that make us see and hear and touch and feel all these things.

B

1. Who were the first occupants of the northern Caribbean?
2. Who were the next occupants of the Caribbean region?
3. Give four examples of ways in which these early Caribbean people found the conch shell useful.
4. What is the fotuto?
5. Give three examples of ways in which Caribbean people continued to use the conch shell.

C Work in groups of three or four. Find out more about the conch. Are there ways in which the conch and its shell are still useful? Find out whether there are any Tainos left in the Caribbean. If so, where do they live and what do they do? Make short notes on your research. Present your notes to the class.

Short forms

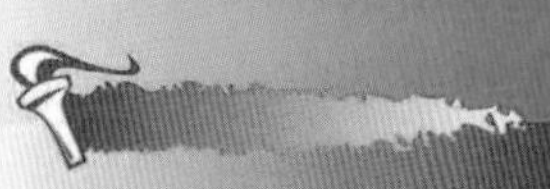

You can join two words when one of them is **not**.

Two words	Short form
is not	isn't
was not	wasn't
does not	doesn't
has not	hasn't

Notice that the apostrophe ' stands for the **o** which has been left out of **not**.

We can also use the ' to join **is** to another word.

Two words	Short form
he is	he's
she is	she's
it is	it's
who is	who's
that is	that's
what is	what's
where is	where's
there is	there's

Remember that the apostrophe ' stands for the **i** of **is** which has been left out.

A Write out these sentences, joining the two words in bold type.

1. Gary says **he is** too busy to play.
2. I think **that is** a lovely dress.
3. Carol is tall, and **she is** pretty, too.
4. Thank goodness **it is** a fine day.
5. We cannot work if **there is** so much noise.
6. I can guess **what is** in the box.
7. I wonder **who is** going to the party tonight.
8. **It is** not raining now.
9. **Where is** the library book I borrowed?
10. I know **there is** another way to do this sum.

Animal noises

- I bark
- I crow
- I cluck
- I bleat
- I grunt
- I bray
- I moo
- I meow

A Write the verb that tells us the sound the animal makes.

1. sheep ______
2. pigs ______
3. dogs ______
4. cows ______
5. donkeys ______
6. cockerels ______
7. hens ______
8. cats ______

B Fill each space with the name of the creature or the name of the noise it makes.

1. The boys were up before the ________ started crowing.
2. They heard the cows ________ in the field.
3. A strange dog was ________ at them.
4. The cat was ________ because she had hurt her paw.
5. The ________ bleated as the sheepdog rounded them up.
6. The ________ grunted as he ate his food.
7. Robert's brown ________ clucked after it lay an egg.
8. Then the loud braying of a ________ woke up the baby.

C Find out about sheepdogs and the work they do. Find out which countries in the Caribbean farm sheep. What are the sheep used for?

Sorting out the story

A The five pictures on this page tell a story. First, look closely at each picture. Figure out what is taking place in each. Then put the pictures in order, to tell the story. After you have put them in order, number them one to five. Next, write two or three sentences about each picture. You can give the people in the story names, if you wish. Find a good title for the story. Put it at the top of the page and underline it.
Work alone or with a partner. Your teacher will tell you which.

POLICE
STATION

POLICE
STATION

Verbs: subjects and verbs agree (1)

In the simple present tense, subjects and verbs agree.
To find the subject ask "Who or what?" before the verb.

Sally likes pawpaws.

What is the verb? Likes.
Who likes pawpaws? Sally
The noun Sally is the subject.
Sally is **one person**, so the noun Sally is **singular**.

The girls like pawpaws.
What is the verb? Likes.
Who like pawpaws? The girls.
The noun girls is the subject.
The noun girls is **more than one**, so it is **plural**.

I like	we like
you like	you like
he, she, it likes	they like

When the subject is one person or thing, add **-s** to the root verb.
When the subject is more than one person or thing, the root verb stays the same.

Singular subject and verb	Plural subject and verb
The boy does.	The boys do.
The girl goes.	The girls go.
The child puts.	The children put.
The dog runs.	The dogs run.
The horse pulls.	The horses pull.
The monkey plays.	The monkeys play.
The parson says.	The parsons say.
The swimmer tries.	The swimmers try.
The donkey carries.	The donkeys carry.
The rider hurries.	The riders hurry.

A Copy the sentences and fill in the missing verb.

1. The friends (**go/goes**) off to play cricket.
2. Harry (**try/tries**) to swim.
3. The men (**pull/pulls**) the cart.
4. Mother (**say/says**) no.
5. The students (**do/does**) their homework.
6. The baby (**put/puts**) the toy in her mouth.
7. Father (**hurry/hurries**) home after work.
8. The thief (**run/runs**) from the policeman.
9. The cab drivers (**carry/carries**) the tourists to the airport.
10. The little boys (**play/plays**) in the street.

B Copy the sentences, using the correct form of the verb.

1. The children (**play/plays**) football every day.
2. Mr. de Freitas (**carry/carries**) his umbrella on his arm.
3. Judith (**do/does**) her crocheting every evening.
4. The students (**go/goes**) to school five days a week.
5. Peter (**say/says**) his prayers every night.
6. The old lady (**hurry/hurries**) to catch the bus.
7. Our cat always (**run/runs**) after a mouse.
8. Pearl (**try/tries**) to do all her chores.

C Write twelve sentences, using **he**, **she** or **it** with the singular form of these verbs and six using **they** with the plural form. Do not use **I**, **you** or **we** as the subject. The first one has been done for you.

1. makes make
   He makes beautiful coloured kites.
   They make very good bread pudding.
2. eats eat
3. reads read
4. thinks think
5. walks walk
6. learns learn

Writing letters

9 High Street
Port of Spain
12th October, 2003

Dear Brian,

Next Friday is my birthday and I am going to have a party. Would you like to come?

We will cut the cake at five o'clock and there will be games and dancing afterwards. The party will end at about ten o'clock.

With love from,
Jasmine Singh

Brian Gordon
25 Victoria Terrace
Diego Martin

Pretend that you have been to Jasmine's party. Write a letter to another friend who was not there telling him what the party was like, mention the things you enjoyed the most. Draw an envelope and address it to your friend.

A Read the letter that Jasmine Singh wrote to Brian Gordon, inviting him to her birthday party. Jasmine's mother showed her how to arrange the letter and how to address the envelope.

Pretend you are Brian Gordon and that you have just received this letter from Jasmine Singh. Write a letter to her thanking her for her invitation and telling her that you will be happy to come. Draw an envelope and address it to Jasmine.

Short forms: using the apostrophe

There are short ways to write some pairs of words.

has not hasn't
he is he's

The apostrophe can also join these pairs.

Long form	Short form
I am	I'm
you are	you're
we are	we're
they are	they're
here is	here's
how is	how's

The apostrophe shows that one or more letters have been missed out.

A Rewrite these sentences, replacing the short forms in bold type with the two words that were joined by the apostrophe.

1. **Where's** this place, Dad?
2. **It's** a lunch counter, son.
3. **What's** in the sandwiches at this place, Dad?
4. **Here's** the sandwich menu: ham, tuna, cheese, and egg salad.
5. **There's** no guava jam and **that's** my favourite.
6. **Who's** that rapping?
7. **It's** Robert and Al. **They're** waiting for you. **We're** all waiting for you.
8. **You're** early. **I'm** not ready yet.
9. Joe is ready and **he's** never early. Sita is ready and **she's** always late.
10. Well, **it's** only two o'clock, so **I'm** not ready. **I'm** sorry but **you're** all going to have to wait.

B Write this passage into your books. Put short forms in place of the two words in bold type.

They are all saying that **we are** going to lose the match. I hope **you are** not saying it too, because **I am** sure **we are** going to win. **Here is** how. **We are** going to wear them down in the first half. **You are** going to run them ragged. **I am** going to wear them down. **We are** all going to give them a workout. When **they are** really beat, **we are** going to go on the attack, and rush the goal again and again. **They are** going to be too weary to defend, and then **we are** going to get goals. **How is** that for a plan?

Comprehension: Roland and the turtle

"Stop! Now! Quickly!" Roland shouted at his mother. "I want to see what it is."

"What are you talking about? I don't see anything except four men carrying a table," she answered. Mrs. Ramir stopped suddenly beside the four men on the sidewalk.

"You call *that* a table?" said Roland. "That's a turtle. It's the largest turtle I've ever seen."

Roland was out of the car in a flash.

"Where did you get it? Why have you tied it up? What are you going to do with it?" he asked.

"Easy, young man. One question at a time," the tallest man said.

They tried to fasten the ropes around the turtle. His cracked brown back was as big as a small table. His eyes were bright and clear. He stretched his thick scaly neck from side to side as if he were trying to escape.

"My goodness," said Mrs. Ramir. "This chap must be three hundred years old."

Suddenly the turtle twisted his neck around. He flapped one leg with all his might. It hit the man who was holding it. The man, shouting in pain, let go. The turtle fell to the ground.

"Run," shouted Roland. "Run for your life. Don't let them get you again, old boy!"

Grace Walker Gordon

A Write down the words from List A. Find a word or phrase from List B that has the same meaning.

A	B
in a flash	get away
fasten	covered with scales
stretched	very quickly
scaly	turned
escape	tie firmly
twisted	pushed out

B

1. What did Roland's mother think the turtle was?
2. Why did the man tell Roland "One question at a time?"
3. Why did the men try to fasten the ropes around the turtle?
4. Describe the turtle.
5. What do you think the men were going to do with the turtle?
6. Why do you think Roland wanted the turtle to escape?
7. What kind of person is Roland? How can you tell?

C Read these sentences and pick out the six adjectives. Put the words in alphabetical order. Then use each one in a short sentence of your own.

The turtle's back was as big as a small table. His eyes were bright and clear. He stretched his thick scaly neck from side to side as if he were trying to escape.

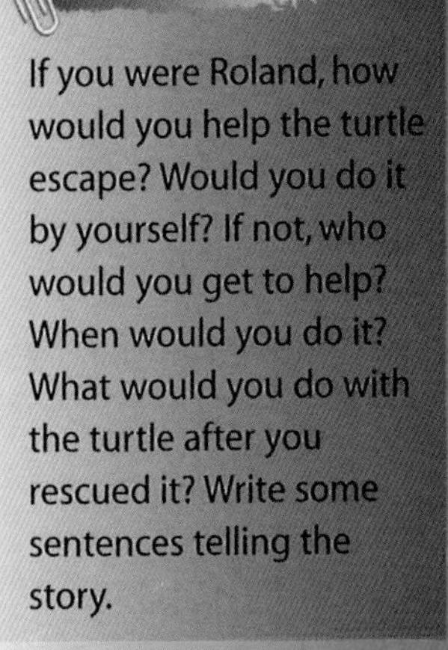

If you were Roland, how would you help the turtle escape? Would you do it by yourself? If not, who would you get to help? When would you do it? What would you do with the turtle after you rescued it? Write some sentences telling the story.

Pronouns

A pronoun is a word that is used instead of a noun.

Hal ran to get the bus but **Hal** did not run fast enough.
Hal ran to get the bus but **he** did not run fast enough.

Instead of repeating the noun **Hal**, we use the pronoun **he**.

Look at these pronouns.

Singular	Plural
he, she, it	they

When I speak **about** myself alone, I say **I**.
When I speak **to** another person, I say **you**.

MARY Mom, **I** have to ask **you** something.
MUM **You** do? Okay. How can **I** help **you**?

When Mary speaks to her Mum, she says **you**.

A Rewrite these sentences in your books, using **he**, **she**, **it**, or **they** in place of the nouns in bold type.

1. The wind almost blew Sandra off the porch so **Sandra** quickly went inside.
2. Sam and Pam felt the rain and **Sam and Pam** started to walk faster.
3. Slowly, the ball began to roll down the hill and then **the ball** rolled faster and faster.
4. When the bull saw the red flag, **the bull** mooed loudly.
5. When the cows heard the bull mooing, **the cows** started mooing too.
6. Peter worked so hard that **Peter** almost fell asleep standing up.

B Complete the passage by choosing **I** or **you** from the words in bold type. Copy it into your books.

"(**I/You**) can't believe that (**I/you**) said something so unkind. (**I/You**) helped (**I/you**) with your homework. (**I/You**) found the library book that (**I/you**) lost. (**I/You**) made lemonade when (**I/you**) were feeling thirsty. And now (**I/You**) say that (**I/you**) am selfish."

MARY Hi, Sam. Hi Pam. Are **you** still going to the movies?

SAM AND PAM Yes, **we** are. Are **you** coming?

When Mary speaks to her friends, Sam and Pam, she says **you** if she doesn't use their names.

When she speaks **about** her friends **and herself** she says **we**.

You and **we** are pronouns.

When they replace nouns that are the subject of the verb, we use the pronouns **I, you, he, she, it, we, you, they**. Because of this, we call them **subject pronouns**.

Subject pronouns

Singular	Plural
I	we
you	you
he, she, it	they

C Read the dialogue below. Copy it carefully into your books. Use the pronouns from the table on the left to fill the gaps.

MARY Mum, Sam and Pam are going to the movies. May _____ go too?

MUM Have _____ watered the beans that _____ planted for your science project?

MARY Aw, Mum. Must _____ water the beans every day?

MUM The beans are plants, dear. If _____ don't get water, _____ won't grow. This morning, _____ saw one little plant and _____ looked almost dead.

MARY Well, Sam and Pam are going to meet me here. Sam said _____ would come at three, and Pam said _____ would come at ten past three. Then _____ will all take the bus to town.

MUM That's fine. Just be careful on the bus, and remember that _____ all need to be home before six.

Opposites: using the prefix un–

A prefix is one or more syllables placed at the beginning of a word to change its meaning. We can give a word an opposite meaning by putting the prefix **un–** before it.

A Write the opposites of these verbs by putting the prefix **un–** before them.

- block
- curl
- roll
- cover
- plug
- leash
- wind
- buckle
- do
- chain

B Choose any five of the words you have made and use them in sentences of your own.

C Copy these sentences, adding **un–** to the adjectives in bold type to give them the opposite meaning.

1. The new driveway is quite **even**.
2. It will be **safe** for the children to ride their bikes.
3. The mangoes were **ripe**.
4. The shopkeeper was **fair** in dealing with his customers.
5. The old man's steps were **steady**.
6. His wife's steps were also **sure**.
7. Ethel was always **pleasant** to her classmates.
8. Her sister Ann was also very **friendly**.
9. The doctor said that Martin was a **healthy** boy.
10. His plan was very **wise**.

Collections

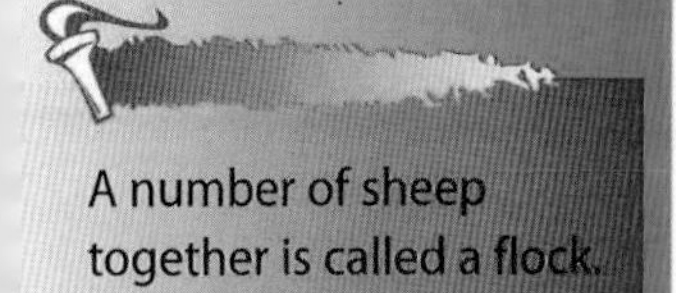

A number of sheep together is called a flock. A number of stars together is called a cluster.

- a bunch of flowers
- a brood of chickens
- a chest of drawers
- a cluster of stars
- a crowd of people
- a flight of steps
- a flock of birds
- a clutch of eggs
- a grove of trees
- a hive of bees
- a herd of cattle
- a pack of wolves
- a pod of whales
- a shoal (or school) of fishes

A Write the word that will fill each gap.

1. A ______ of steps led to the cabin.
2. A large ______ of pigeons flew over the town.
3. Our milk comes from a ______ of Jersey cows.
4. A ______ of wolves went hunting in the forest.
5. When Ann was in St Lucia, she saw a ______ of whales swimming past the island.
6. A ______ of people gathered to welcome the Prime Minister.
7. The clothes were kept in an old ______ of drawers.
8. The boys hid in a ______ of trees and waited for the birds.
9. Father went to his ______ of bees to get honey.
10. When my aunt was in hospital my uncle took her a lovely ______ of flowers.
11. A ______ of fishes swam past our boat.
12. Each hen was sitting on her own ______ of eggs.

B Make up an echo poem about collections of animals. In an echo poem, you repeat each line, adding a word or phrase for emphasis. The word in this poem is **see**.

A pod of whales.
See, a pod of whales.
A hive of bees.
See, a hive of bees.
A bunch of flowers.
See, a bunch of flowers.

Occupations

- stewardess
- tailor
- lawyer
- hairdresser
- security guard
- author
- lifeguard
- waiter
- sailor
- gardener
- window cleaner
- porter

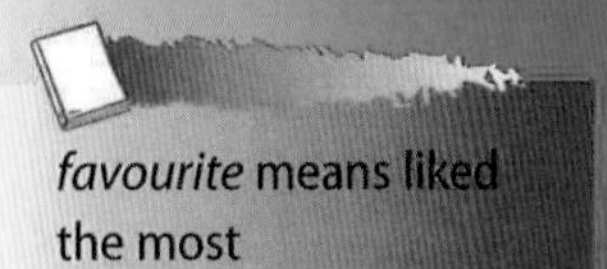

favourite means liked the most

A Use the words in the list on the left to name each person. Number them 1 to 8 as in the pictures.

B Write the missing words. The list will help you.

1. The ________ carried the baby off the plane.
2. The ________ helped her to find her luggage.
3. The ________ jumped from the window he was washing and grabbed the thief.
4. Then the ________ rushed out from the bank and put him in handcuffs.
5. Jane went to the ________ for a hair cut.
6. Ben went off to find a book by his favourite ________ .
7. The old ________ made the King's clothes.
8. The suntanned ________ worked on the SS Sunrise.

Opposites: adjectives

Look at this list of adjectives that show opposites.

dull	sharp
back	front
glad	sorry
sour	sweet
dark	light
long	short
poor	rich
fast	slow
noisy	quiet
easy	difficult

A Choose the opposite of the word in bold type from the list on the left to fill each space.

1. a fast train **slow**
2. a _____ pencil **dull**
3. a _____ sky **dark**
4. a _____ seat **back**
5. a _____ story **long**
6. a _____ orange **sweet**
7. a _____ street **quiet**
8. a _____ man **poor**
9. a _____ task **easy**
10. to be _____ **glad**

B Fill each gap with the opposite of the word in bold.

1. The first test was **easy** but the second was _____ .
2. We are going to paint the **front** fence and the _____ door of our house.
3. He was _____ when his cousin came but **sorry** when he left.
4. The knife was _____ a week ago, but now it's too **blunt** to cut cheese!
5. He tied the _____ cord to the **long** one.
6. It was **quiet** in the church but _____ outside.
7. Ten years ago he was _____ . Now he is **rich.**
8. She wore a **dark** blue gown and _____ blue gloves.
9. The clock was ten minutes **fast** but it's now _____.
10. Some people like lemonade to be **sweet**, but I like it _____ .

Comprehension: Pimento Walk

Pimento Walk was a great grove of pimento trees. It was a favourite feeding ground for many birds. White-wings, baldpates and pigeons especially liked to feed there. While the boys were on their way, they broke branches from the trees they passed. They covered themselves all over with the branches. Soon they looked like walking trees. Only their hands were free.

When they reached the pimento grove, Tommy gave a sign. At this, they separated. Each boy went to a different place. They kept very still and waited. Then the birds began to appear.

They came in flocks from the west. Into the pimento grove they flew for their morning feed. The young Maroon warriors shot at the birds with their backs to the sun. Their bows sang. Their arrows flew as fast as their fingers could reach the quivers on their backs. Only a few of the arrows missed. In a short time there were many birds on the ground for the cooking pots of Mountain Top Village.

Adapted from *The Young Warriors* by Vic Reid

this was bad

A Find these words in the passage. Then choose meaning that matches the way the word is used.

1. Grove means a) ground b) groovy c) group.
2. Favourite means a) well supplied b) good looking c) well liked.
3. Separated means a) went to different places b) marched away c) left.
4. In flocks means a) in groups b) in flying formations c) in sudden bursts.
5. Quivers means a) feathers b) arrows c) cases for arrows.
6. Warriors means a) fighters b) chiefs c) worried people.

B

1. What was Pimento Walk?
2. Why were the boys going to Pimento Walk?
3. What did the boys do while they were on their way there? Why?
4. Why did they leave their hands free?
5. Why do you think each boy went to a different place?
6. Why did the boys keep very still while they waited?
7. Why do you think they shot at the birds with their backs to the sun?
8. What were the boys going to do with the birds?
9. Why do you think the passage says the boys were warriors?
10. Explain what *their bows sang* means.
11. Re-read the passage. Select any three adjectives and use them in sentences.

C Copy the passage, changing the past tense to the present tense. Use a dictionary if you need to. Underline each of the verbs. The first two sentences are done for you.

Pimento Walk is a great grove of pimento trees. It is a favourite feeding ground for many birds.

Animals

- bear
- lion
- donkey
- hedgehog
- kangaroo
- mongoose
- camel
- giraffe
- elephant
- squirrel

A List the numbers from 1 to 10. Then write the names of these animals beside the numbers.

B Write the name of the animal that will complete each sentence. The names are in the list.

1. The _________ is covered with sharp spines and can roll itself into a ball when attacked.
2. The _________ has a long trunk and strong tusks.
3. The _________ has a hump on its back and can carry people and goods across the desert.
4. The _________ has a patterned skin and a very long neck.
5. The _________ has a bushy tail that curls over its back.
6. The _________ is a cunning animal that steals chickens.
7. The _________ is called The King of Beasts. Its loud roar frightens many animals.
8. The _________ is a stubborn animal with very long ears. It is sometimes called an ass.
9. The _________ has strong hind legs that enable it to move forward in great leaps.
10. A _________ has a thick coat and strong claws. It can hug a person to death.

Groups or categories

An orange is a **fruit**. So is a plum and so is a cherry. They all belong to the same **group**. They are all fruits.

A cabbage is a **vegetable**.

A rose is a **flower**.

A doll is a **toy**.

- bird
- fish
- toy
- tree
- tool
- fruit
- flower
- insect
- animal
- vegetable
- colour
- day

category means set, group, collection

A Copy these sentences, putting the correct group name in each space.

1. A rattle is a ______ .
2. A banana is a ______ .
3. A herring is a ______ .
4. A cedar is a ______ .
5. A donkey is an ______ .
6. A bee is an ______ .
7. A turnip is a ______ .
8. A dahlia is a ______ .
9. A parrot is a ______ .
10. A hammer is a ______ .

B Draw four columns in your books, like these. Then put the words below in the correct columns.

Fruits	Fishes	Vegetables	Tools
lettuce	cabbage	screwdriver	onion
hammer	lime	snapper	salmon
orange	grouper	plum	hatchet
carrot	spade	banana	barracuda
herring	cherry	spanner	pumpkin

C In each column below there is one word that does not belong to the same group as the others.
Write the word that does not fit.

1.	2.	3.
palm	blue	mango
teak	bright	orange
greenheart	black	carrot
rose	yellow	lime
cedar	green	grapefruit

4.	5.	6.
cow	Christmas	orchid
goat	Friday	hibiscus
sheep	Wednesday	coconut
moth	Monday	ixora
horse	Thursday	bougainvillea

Verbs: subjects and verbs agree (2)

In the simple present tense, subjects and verbs agree.
The verb tells the action.
To find the subject ask "Who or what?" before the verb.

I sing with the choir.

What is the verb? Sing.
Who sings? **I.**
The pronoun **I** is the subject.
I am **one person**, so the pronoun I is **singular**.

You sing in the choir, Mary.
Who sings? **You**. (one person, Mary)
The pronoun **you** is the subject.
In this case, the pronoun you is **one person**, so it is **singular**.

Subject: I	Subject: you
I do	You do
I go	You go
I put	You put
I pull	You pull
I play	You play
I say	You say
I try	You try
I carry	You carry
I hurry	You hurry

For verbs in the simple present tense, when the subject is I or you and therefore singular, do not add anything to the root verb.

A Rewrite these sentences, choosing the correct form of the verb from each pair.

1. You (**have/has**) a heavy school bag, Ann.
2. Every day I (**carry/carries**) home one as heavy as this.
3. I (**put/puts**) heavy things in this wagon and I (**pull/pulls**) them.
4. You (**am/are**) very smart, Errol.
5. I (**try/tries**) very hard at Math, Dan.
6. You (**say/says**) that, Roger. That's not what I (**say/says**).
7. You (**know/knows**) nothing about it!
8. But I (**do/does**) because I (**watch/watches**) you doing your Math homework!

B Copy this passage into your books. It is a note that Roger wrote to Dan. He got some things wrong! Correct all the words that are in bold type with the right form of the verb. The first one is done for you.

> You **believes** that you **knows** everything, Roger. I **gets** tired of it. You **bosses** me around all the time. But you never **sees** when I **does** anything right. You **thinks** that I **feels** good when you **says** bad things about me? Well, I **tells** you, I **suffers** from your unkind comments. I really **dislikes** you sometimes.

You believe that you know everything, Roger.

The months of the year

A A year in which February has 29 days is known as a Leap Year. Look at the calendar, and then answer these questions in your books.

1. How many months are there in the year?
2. Which month has the shortest name?
3. Which three months have names ending with **–ember**?
4. Which month has the longest name?
5. Which month has the fewest days?
6. In which month does your birthday come?
7. In which month does Christmas come?
8. Which four months do not have the letter **r** in them?

B We can write the names of most of the months in a short way. Copy these short forms and learn them.

1.	January	Jan.
2.	February	Feb.
3.	March	Mar.
4.	August	Aug.
5.	September	Sept.
6.	October	Oct.
7.	November	Nov.
8.	December	Dec.

Adverbs

Andrew tiptoed quietly from the room.

The word quietly tells **how** Andrew left the room. This word is formed by adding **–ly** to **quiet**.

When **–ly** is added to words ending with **y**, this letter is first changed to **i**.

clumsy clums**ily**
hasty hast**ily**

A Add **–ly** to each of these words, then use each one in a short sentence.

- quick
- kind
- calm
- neat
- sad
- quiet
- safe
- proud
- bold
- fond

B Change the **y** at the end to **i** and add **–ly** to these words. Use each one in a short sentence.

- easy
- lucky
- busy
- heavy
- sleepy
- angry
- noisy
- steady
- greedy
- hungry

C The word that fills each space below is formed by adding **–ly** to the word in bold type. Write the nine words.

1. The flames spread so ________ that the house was soon burnt to the ground. (**quick**)
2. All the boys were working ________ . (**busy**)
3. The ship arrived ________ after a stormy voyage. (**safe**)
4. The snail crept ________ along the garden path. (**slow**)
5. The old man nodded his head ________. (**sleepy**)
6. It is raining too ________ for you to go out. (**heavy**)
7. The young mother looked ________ at her baby. (**proud**)
8. Sandra wrote the letter very ________. (**neat**)
9. Philip jumped over the wall quite ________. (**easy**)
10. She ________ kissed her grandmother goodbye. (**fond**)

Using quotation or speech marks

Look at this sentence.
"This orange is sour," said Robert.
The words spoken by Robert were **This orange is sour.**

Notice the speech marks come before the first word spoken **"This** and after the last word spoken **sour,"** .

Also notice that the speech marks come after the comma: **sour,"** .

The speech marks also come after a question mark: **?"** .

"Is the orange sour**?"** asked Robert.

A Copy these sentences in your books. Put in the speech marks.

1. Please have a slice of cake, said Mrs. Evans.
2. I can see you, shouted Evelyn.
3. Come here, Spot, said the little boy to his dog.
4. I don't want to go to bed yet, said Sandra with a pout.
5. Hurry up, Linda, or you'll be late, said her father.
6. Be quiet, the baby's sleeping, whispered Jennifer's mother.

B Copy these sentences into your books. Put in the speech marks.

1. Are you tired? asked the teacher.
2. Miss, will you send me home if I say yes? Sue asked in reply.
3. Please, Mummy, may I have an apple? begged Carl.
4. Have you been good today? inquired Mummy, with a smile.
5. Won't you give to our building fund, please? the two boys pleaded.
6. Can you promise me that you won't spend the money on sweets? asked Mr. Hill.

C Write three sentences of your own in which you use speech marks to show the words people speak. Remember, you must use the exact words and you must say who speaks them.

Using as and has

We use **as** to compare things.
Sam is **as** tall as Alex.

We also use it to mean at the time that.
As the star fell, I made a wish.

And we use it to mean because.
I visit my aunt often, **as** she is lonely.

Has is part of the verb **to have**.
The boy **has** the bat.
The ball **has** a hole in it.

Has is also used as a helping word to show past time.
Ron **has** done his work.

A Use **as** or **has** to fill the spaces. Copy the sentences into your books.

1. Ben wanted to go to the game so he worked _______ hard _______ he could to do his chores.
2. Nandi cannot go _______ she _______ not finished her chores.
3. Joy ________ a lump ________ big ________ an egg on her forehead.
4. _______ the sun went behind the clouds, the rain began to pour.
5. "It _______ not rained _______ hard _______ this for ages," said Sue.

B Copy this passage into your books. Choose **has** or **as** to put in each space.

" I think Fred _______ done a fine job of cleaning up," Mr Wong said." ______ he ______ worked so hard, he can go home early." Fred was ______ happy ______ could be. ______ soon ____ he heard the news, he was out of the door. But he was not ______ quick ______ he should have been. ______ he ran towards the gate, two bullies from his class stood in his way.

What do you think happened to Fred? Write some sentences to finish the story.

Comprehension: How the Pelican got its beak

One day, the Pelican, the Carite, the Boobie and the Corbeau were sunning themselves. They were on the rocks at Point Galera. The Carite Bird was boasting about how many fish he had caught for the day. The Pelican said to him, "Carite, you are always saying how fast you fly. You are always saying how well you dive. I don't think you would be able to fish so well if you did not have that beak."

"Go away!" the Carite Bird said. "You are only saying this because your wings are larger than mine. They are stronger too. Yet you cannot do what I can. You are jealous."

"I am not jealous," the Pelican said. "And I am not saying that you do not fly and dive very well. But I don't think that you do so better than anyone else. I still say it is your beak."

The Corbeau joined in. "I agree with Pelican. You catch more fish because of your beak. It has a hook on the end," he said.

"You are both jealous of me," Carite answered, vexed. "You are only trying to insult me by talking about the hook on my beak. I still say that I can fly and dive better than any of you."

"Well," said the Corbeau, "you really are very pig-headed. But I have an idea. You say you can fly and dive so well that you do not need your beak. So lend it to the Pelican. Then you borrow his. Then if he does not catch any fish and you continue to catch fish we shall believe you."

The Pelican was amazed by this idea. He held his breath, hardly daring to hope that the Carite Bird would agree.

Nine Folk Tales by Eaulin Ashtine

A Write down the words and phrases in List A. Find a word or phrase from List B that has the same meaning.

A	B
boasting	stubborn
jealous	barely having the courage
vexed	be rude to
insult	showing off
pig headed	envious
hardly daring	angry

B

1. What was the Carite Bird boasting about?
2. According to Pelican and Corbeau, what helped Carite to fish so well?
3. Who had larger and stronger wings?
4. How did Carite feel about what the others said?
5. Write out the sentence in which the Carite states the two things he can do better than the others. Begin, The Carite said. Use speech marks and commas.
6. Write out the sentences in which Corbeau suggests a way for Carite to prove his claim. Begin, Corbeau remarked. Use speech marks and commas.
7. What would Carite prove if he caught fish with Pelican's beak?
8. What would be proved if Pelican did not catch fish with Carite's beak?
9. How do you think the story ends? The title and the picture give clues.

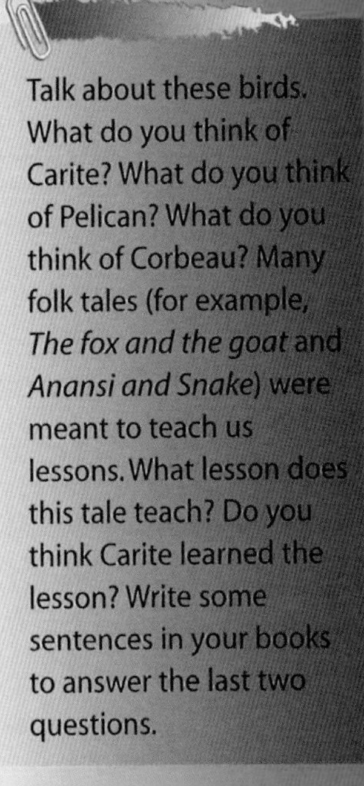

Talk about these birds. What do you think of Carite? What do you think of Pelican? What do you think of Corbeau? Many folk tales (for example, *The fox and the goat* and *Anansi and Snake*) were meant to teach us lessons. What lesson does this tale teach? Do you think Carite learned the lesson? Write some sentences in your books to answer the last two questions.

Verbs: more verbs that change to show past time

Present time
We **drive** slowly because the traffic is heavy.

Past time
We **drove** slowly yesterday because the traffic was heavy.

Present	Past
build	built
choose	chose
drive	drove
feed	fed
grow	grew
leave	left
ride	rode
say	said
speak	spoke
steal	stole
sweep	swept
tear	tore
wake	woke
win	won

a *bouquet* is a bunch of flowers

Learn the verbs in the list on the left, and then answer the questions.

A Copy this column. Fill the blanks.

	Present	Past
1.	_______	built
2.	_______	left
3.	_______	swept
4.	_______	grew
5.	_______	said
6.	_______	rode
7.	_______	spoke
8.	choose	_______
9.	drive	_______
10.	feed	_______
11.	tear	_______
12.	wake	_______
13.	steal	_______
14.	win	_______

B Copy these sentences into your books using the best words to fill the gaps.

1. He _______ to the park on his new bicycle.
2. At the park, he _______ bread to the pigeons.
3. The boy _______ his shirt when he fell down the stairs and hurt his arm.
4. His mother quickly_______ to the school and took him to the doctor.
5. The gardener _______ some beautiful roses in the rich dark soil.

6. He ________ the prettiest ones to cut as a bouquet for my sister.
7. Yesterday I ________ to the carpenter on the phone.
8. He told me that he ________ the hen house in two days and ________ up all the rubbish afterwards.
9. We ________ two tickets to go to the zoo in the contest.
10. We saw two cute bear cubs that yawned and stretched like babies when they ________.
11. The burglar broke into the shop and ________ money from the till.
12. He ________ five dollars and a note that ________ thanks.

Poetry: Catch a Little Rhyme

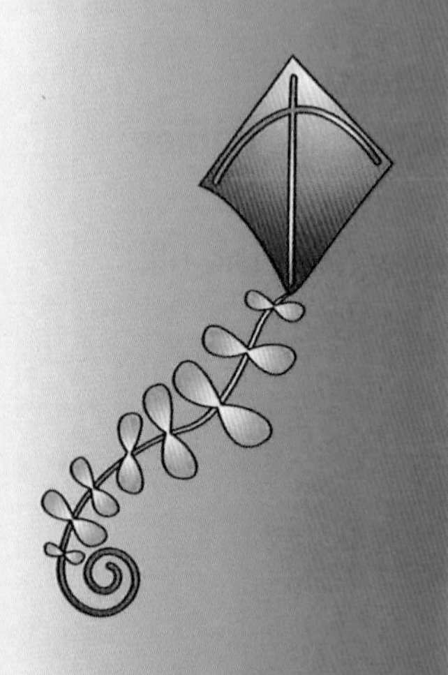

Catch a Little Rhyme

Once upon time
I caught a little rhyme

I set it on the floor
but it ran right out the door

I chased it on my bicycle
but it melted to an icicle

I scooped it up in my hat
but it turned into a cat

I caught it by the tail
but it stretched into a whale

I followed it in a boat
but it changed into a goat

When I fed it tin and paper
it became a tall skyscraper

Then it grew into a kite
and flew far out of sight…

Eve Merriam

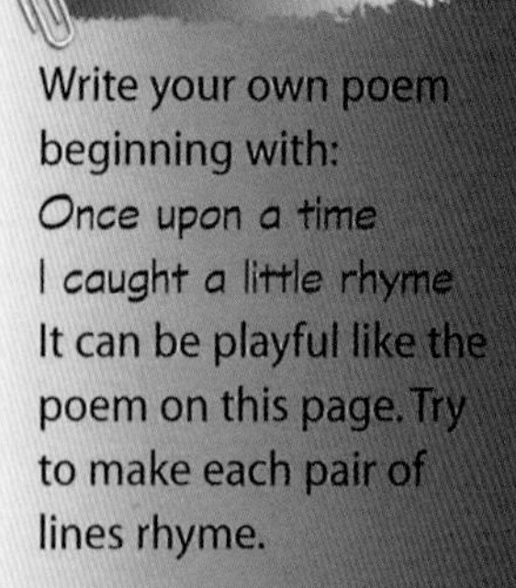

Write your own poem beginning with:
Once upon a time
I caught a little rhyme
It can be playful like the poem on this page. Try to make each pair of lines rhyme.

A Read the poem quietly, and then read it together aloud several times.

B Is it possible to catch a rhyme? If so, explain how. Does the poem make complete sense, a bit of sense, or no sense at all? Is it serious, or is it funny?

Abbreviated or short forms

There is a short way of writing some words.

Avenue	Ave.
Doctor	Dr.
Honourable	Hon.
Missis	Mrs.
Mister	Mr.
Road	Rd.
Square	Sq.
Street	St.
Terrace	Terr.

Instead of writing a person's given name or names in full we often write only the first letter, or **initial**. We write it as a capital and put a full stop after it.

Edward Marsh E. Marsh
Abe John Bond A. J. Bond

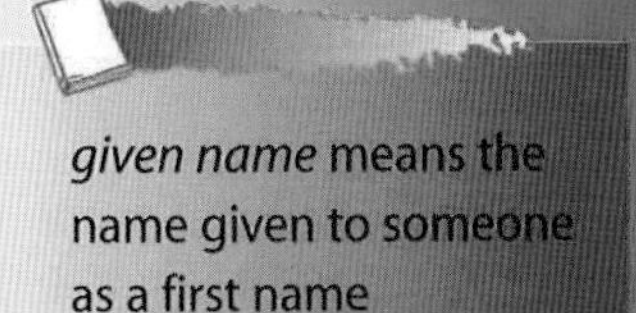

given name means the name given to someone as a first name

A Write each of these the short way.

1. Doctor Smith
2. High Street
3. Mister Lee
4. Magnolia Terrace
5. Missis Bond
6. Bush Avenue
7. Victoria Square
8. Redlands Road

B Draw envelopes in your books and write these names and addresses, using initials and the short forms you have learnt.

1. Mister Tyrone Worrel, of 12 Water Street, Georgetown.
2. Missis Nandrani Persaud, of 9 Lombard Road, Bel Air.
3. Miss Eslyn Yvonne Braithwaite, of 16 Park Terrace, San Fernando.
4. Doctor Philip Christopher Rodrigues, of 23 Main Avenue, Kingston 7.
5. Honourable Alexander James Montague of 2 Nevis Drive, Sea Sands Park.

Building a story

These are three important things about a story.

1. A story has **characters**. The characters are the people in the story.
2. A story takes place in a **setting**. The setting is the place where the story happens.
3 It has a **beginning**, **middle** and an **end**. This means something happens in the story to change the way the characters were at the beginning so that they are different in the end. The middle of the story tells about this change.

Sometimes we confuse a **story** and a **series of events**. In a series of events, **things happen** to people but they do not make the people change. In a story, the **characters change** in some important way. They may become happier, or sadder, or wiser or more generous or more set in their ways, but they change somehow.

A Read these passages, then talk about whether each one is a story or a series of events. Ask these questions:

- Who are the characters?
- What is the setting?
- Does anything happen to change the way the characters were at the beginning so that they are different in the end?

1. Deli and Ann read for an hour or so. Then they put on their pajamas, washed their faces and cleaned their teeth and went to bed. They slept very soundly. Next morning they got up. They bathed and dressed. Then they went downstairs and ate a big breakfast. Afterwards, they went outside to do their chores.

2. Deli's Mum warned her not to eat too many oranges. One day she snuck into the kitchen and ate about two dozen. She felt really sick and when she looked, she had turned a bright orange. Suddenly a little old lady appeared on the kitchen table. She was tiny, beautiful, and round, and she was bright orange. "I won't tell you not to eat oranges, Deli," she said, "but if you eat too many again, you'll become an orange person, and you'll have to come and live with us." Then she smiled and disappeared. Deli never ate too many oranges after that.

B Write a story of your own. Before you begin, make a list of who the characters are, where the story is going to take place and what happens to change the characters. Illustrate your stories and read them in class.

Riddles

What am I?

1. I never come up
   where I go down
   and I always go
   the same way round.

2. Room full
   Hall full,
   Can't get
   A spoon full.

3. You don't like it when I come
   You are happy when I'm gone
   But without me the world
   Would be cracked and brown.

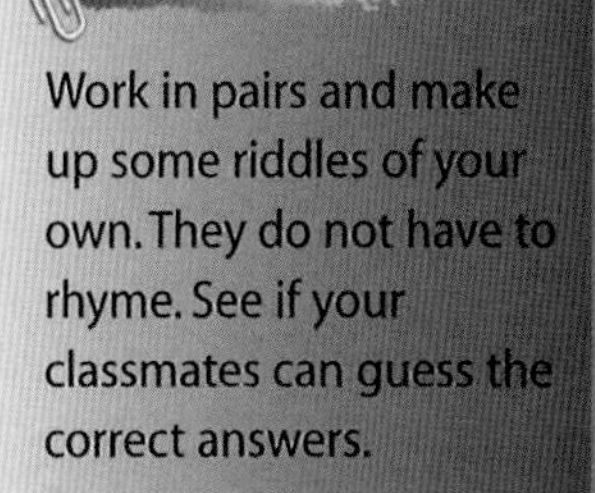

1. the sun, 2. smoke, 3. the rain

Writing book reviews

A book review is a good way to advertise a new book or remind people of a good one written long ago. A review can tell your friends or classmates about a good (or bad) book. Here is a review by a person who liked the book that they read.

Harry Potter and the Philosopher's Stone
by J. K. Rowling
Reviewed by Love To Read

This is a book about how a boy finds out that he is really a wizard. The hero's name is Harry Potter. An evil wizard comes to Harry's house when he is a baby. The wizard kills his parents. Harry is saved. He goes to live with his aunt and uncle and cousin who are mean to him. But then he gets to go to Hogwarts, which is the best wizard school. He makes friends with Ron and Hermione and they have many adventures. I won't tell about them or it will spoil the fun.

There are many exciting parts. One is when Harry's team plays in a game where everyone rides on a broom. A bad Professor puts a spell on Harry's broom. It bumps about and nearly throws Harry off. There are some scary parts, too. When Harry and his friends try to get past the huge, horrible dog and their magic doesn't work right, it's scary.

Harry's world is full of magical people and things. The big mystery is of course about the powerful Philosopher's Stone. If you have it you can live forever. When the stone gets into the wrong hands, Harry and his friends must fight to make things right. They have to go through many adventures to do this.

I really like this book. It has adventure and magic and mystery. It is exciting and scary. I think boys and girls would like it. I found it in the school library.

A Choose a book that you have read and enjoyed recently. Start the review by writing the name of the book and the name of the author. Underline the title of the book, or write it all in capital letters. Check to see that you spell the names of the book and author correctly. Put your own name on the second line, after "Reviewed by".

The review should tell:

- What the story is about
- Who the main character is/main characters are
- What parts of the story are most exciting/happiest/funniest/saddest/scariest
- Who you think would like the story, for example, people who like adventure or mystery or sports or history
- Where you can find the book.

B Edit your review. Check whether you have used capital letters in the right places. Check the punctuation. If you are not sure of the correct spelling of any words, use your dictionary to check. Make sure that the author's name and the name of the book are correct. (You should talk about why this is important.)

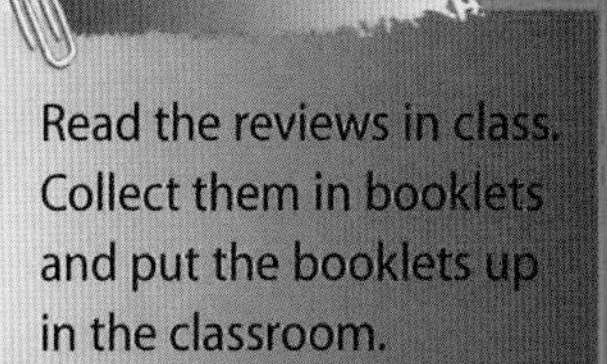

Using took and taken

Take is an **irregular** verb. It is irregular because it **does not follow the rule** to add **–ed** to show the past tense. Instead, it changes the form (or shape) of the root verb.

To show the past time of **take** we use **took**.

Alice **took** the book home.

The word **took** does not need a helping word.

We can also use **has taken**, **have taken** and **had taken** for past time. The word taken always needs one of the helping words **has**, **have** or **had**.

Alice **has taken** her book home.
Alice and Max **have taken** their books home.
Alice **had taken** her book home.

A Use **took** or **taken** to fill each space.

1. I have _______ my book.
2. Have you _______ yours?
3. He had _______ my pen.
4. So I _______ his.
5. You _______ care in the last test.
6. And you have _______ care in this one.
7. He has _______ the cricket bats.
8. We have _______ the balls.
9. She had _______ her brother to the clinic.
10. After that, she _______ him home.

B Fill each space with **took** or **taken**.

1. She had _______ ill at the cricket match.
2. They _______ her to the hospital.
3. Now the doctor has _______ out her appendix.
4. The thief _______ all the spoons in the house.
5. "Dad!" the children shouted. "Someone has _______ all our spoons!"
6. The police came quickly and now they have _______ the thief to jail.
7. We _______ the shortest time to finish the hundred yards race.
8. We have _______ the shortest time in the last two championships.
9. You have _______ the longest time for this race last year and this year.
10. We don't care since we _______ home the championship cup both times!

Using see, saw and seen

See is an irregular verb. It is irregular because it does not follow the rule to add **–ed** to show the past tense. Instead, it changes the form (or shape) of the root verb.

To show the past time of **see** we use **saw**. The word **saw** does not need a helping word.

Ed **saw** the old fort.

We can also use **has seen**, **have seen** and **had seen** for past time. The word **seen** always needs one of the helping words has, have or had.

Ed **has seen** the old fort. Ed and Al **have seen** the old fort. They **had seen** it once before.

A Use **saw** or **seen** to fill each space.

1. I ______ my report card
2. Al has ______ his too.
3. Have you ______ yours?
4. The boys had ______ the play.
5. The girls had ______ it too.
6. Who ______ the movie?
7. I have not ______ it.
8. Amoy has not ______ it.
9. Ed ______ it long ago.
10. But he ______ it in Miami.

B Choose **saw** or **seen** to finish each sentence. Copy these sentences into your books.

1. I (**saw/seen**) a big stingray last Sunday.
2. It is the biggest stingray I have ever (**saw/seen**).
3. We (**saw/seen**) the accident.
4. We had (**saw/seen**) many accidents before.
5. But we have never (**saw/seen**) such a bad one.
6. Mrs. Fong has not (**saw/seen**) her newest grandchild.
7. She had (**saw/seen**) the other two when they were born.
8. But she has not (**saw/seen**) Clara because she was born abroad.
9. Has anyone (**saw/seen**) my dictionary?
10. I have not (**saw/seen**) it for about a week.

Homophones (3)

You have learned (pages 25 and 39) that words that sound alike but are spelt differently are called **homophones**.

Look at these four pairs of words. Learn to spell each word. Learn the meaning of each.

main **Main** means most important.

mane The long hair on the neck of a horse or a lion is called a **mane**.

meat The flesh of an animal used for food is called **meat**.

meet **Meet** means get together.

pail A **pail** is a kind of bucket.

pale A **pale** colour is a light colour.

sure **Sure** means certain.

shore **Shore** means seashore, coastline, the point where the land meets the sea.

A Choose the correct word from the pair above to complete each sentence.

1. **pale** **pail**
   She was wearing a ______ blue dress.
2. **meat** **meet**
   The ______ was too tough to eat.
3. **sure** **shore**
   Helen was ______ that she had passed the test.
4. **main** **mane**
   The school is on the ______ road.
5. **pale** **pail**
   The ______ was half full of water.
6. **main** **mane**
   The horse had a very long ______ .
7. **sure** **shore**
   The girls looked for seashells along the ______ .
8. **meat** **meet**
   We will ______ you outside the cinema.

Compound words

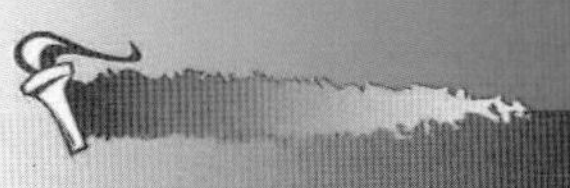

A **compound** word is formed by **joining together** two or more words.

tea + pot = teapot

- armchair
- wheelbarrow
- birdcage
- matchbox
- butterfly
- bulldog
- flowerpot
- lawnmower
- football
- footprint
- dustbin
- hummingbird
- broomstick

A Write all of the words in the list on the left that can be found in the picture below. Then write the two words that make up each compound word.

1. *foot + print = footprint*

B In each line below, join together the two words in bold type to form a compound word. Start with the second word. Use each word you make in a short sentence. Your teacher will tell you whether to write the sentences in your books or take turns saying them in class.

1. a **fish** that is **gold** in colour *goldfish*
2. a **boat** that is driven by a **motor**
3. a **stand** on which a **band** plays
4. a **cloth** that covers a **table**
5. a **fly** that lives in **sand**
6. a **ring** for the **ear**
7. a **weed** that grows in the **sea**
8. a **tray** to hold cigarette **ash**
9. a **pack** worn on the **back**
10. a **fish** with a **shell**

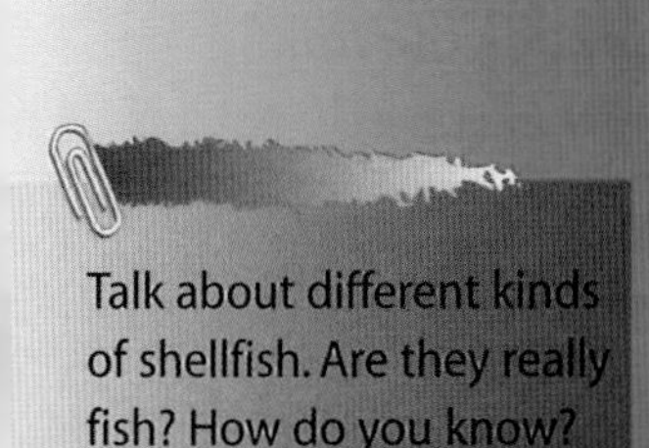

Talk about different kinds of shellfish. Are they really fish? How do you know?

How to make a model of a pig

Here are the things you will need.

- 1 pear-shaped balloon
- newspaper
- soft brown paper
- paste
- card
- paint
- string

Blow up the balloon fairly hard. To keep the air in, tie a knot in the neck. Rub Vaseline® over the balloon. This is so it will slide out easily. Cut the paper into strips. Soak the strips in paste. Leaving a section about 25mm around the neck bare, cover the balloon with strips of newspaper, then brown paper. That way, you can see if you covered the whole balloon each time. Put on about five layers of paper. Then hang the balloon up to dry (Fig. 1).

By now the balloon should look a bit like a pig. Make sure the paper is dry. Untie the neck of the balloon. Take it out of the hole. If it sticks, leave it in. Tuck in the neck so the surface of the pig is smooth. Cover the hole with more paper. Do this till the pig is rounded out (Fig. 2). To make the legs, crumple up brown paper. Paste it to the body with paper strips (Fig. 3). Make a snout in the same way.

Cut the pig's ears from card. Cut tabs along the straight end of the ears. Bend every other tab in a different direction. Paste the tabs onto the pig with paper strips as well (Fig. 4). Use string for the tail. Fray one end of the string. Use strips of paper soaked in paste to attach the frayed end. When dry and firm, the pig can be painted (Fig. 5). Paint quickly. Use the brush lightly. If you don't, the pig will get soggy. You can also varnish the pig.

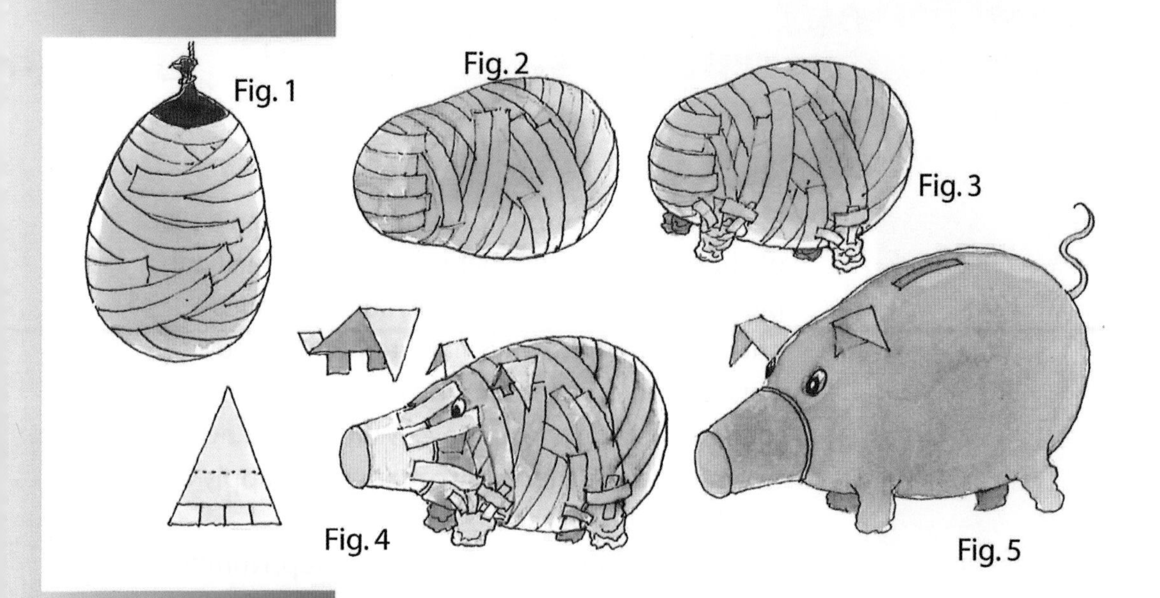

A Select the correct meaning for each of these words as they are used in the passage.

1. Tuck means a) bend b) fold in pleats c) push.
2. Crumple means a) fall apart b) crush c) collapse.
3. Snout means a) pig's beak b) pig's nose c) pig's tail
4. Fray means a) unravel b) wear out c) rub.
5. Soggy means a) damp b) rainy c) very wet.

B

1. Why do you blow up the balloon fairly hard?
2. Why do you leave the section around the neck bare?
3. Explain why you rub Vaseline® over the balloon.
4. Explain why you cover the balloon with strips of newspaper, then brown paper.
5. Why does the balloon have to be dry before you put on the legs and the snout and the ears?
6. Why do you have to paint quickly and use the paintbrush lightly?

Choose something simple that you have made, for example, a sandwich, a drink, a paper aeroplane. Write instructions for how to make it. Use simple sentences and draw diagrams if you wish. Your teacher will tell you if you can work with a partner. Put up your diagrams and instructions in the classroom. Your classmates will tell you if they could make the object by following your instructions.

Writing instructions

A Look at the pictures showing how to clean a pair of shoes. Talk about what is happening in each picture. Why is the child polishing the shoes outside? Do you always have to polish shoes outside and on a table? Why is nothing happening to the shoes in the Picture 4? Why do you need two brushes? Is there any other way to apply the polish? Is a brush the best way?
Write out the instructions, step by step. Number each step. Some pictures show one and others more than one step. You may use as many sentences as you wish. Try to keep your sentences short and clear. Your teacher will tell you whether to work alone or in pairs.

B Edit your instructions. Check spelling. Check whether each sentence starts with a capital letter and ends with a full stop. Check whether the sentences are clear.

C Read each other's instructions, whether you have worked singly or in pairs. Were your instructions clear? Did you miss anything?

Write out the instructions for playing a simple game like Hide and Seek. Use these questions as a guide.

- How many can play?
- What do you need?
- What are the rules?
- What is the first thing that you do?
- What is the next thing, and the thing that follows that?
- How does the game end?

Short forms

The short way of writing **has not** is **hasn't**.
The short way of writing **that is** is **that's**.

In a similar way the word **will** can be added to words and written in a short way.

I will	I'll
you will	you'll
he will	he'll
she will	she'll
we will	we'll
they will	they'll

Remember that the ' shows that the letters **wi** have been left out.

A Write the short form for these words and use them in short sentences.

1. we will
2. he will
3. you will
4. they will
5. I will
6. she will

B Rewrite these sentences using the short form of the two words in bold type.

1. I know **you will** be pleased with your present.
2. Peter says **he will** be at your party.
3. Next time **we will** go by canoe.
4. I promise that **I will** do my best.
5. If Babs is late **she will** be in trouble.
6. The boys say **they will** call on their way over.

C Replace the short forms in the sentences below with the two words that were joined together.

He'll never know if we put stones in the bag. **They'll** be the same weight as the jewellery he stole. By the time he wakes up and finds out, **we'll** be gone. **I'll** sneak over and take up the bag. **You'll** go find some stones. **I'll** wake Betty. **She'll** be the best person to take the jewels out and put the stones in. **She'll** not make any noise. Then **you'll** both tiptoe outside. **I'll** leave last. Then **we'll** run as fast as we can. **We'll** be running for our lives.

Comprehension: The lion and the mouse

A lion was asleep in his den one day. A playful little mouse ran up his paw. Then it ran across his nose. With a start, the lion woke from his nap. As quick as lightning he clapped down his huge paw and caught the frightened little mouse. He was not pleased at being disturbed. Throwing back his head, he roared angrily.

"Please don't kill me," the mouse squealed. "Forgive me this time, please. I promise I will never forget it. One day I may be able to do you a good turn. If so, I promise to repay your kindness."

The lion smiled at thc mousc. He was amused by the thought. How could such a tiny creature ever be able to help him? Still, he lifted his paw. The mouse scampered off.

Later that day, the lion was out hunting. Some men had set a net to catch him. And it did. At once the lion let out a mighty roar. It echoed far and wide. It sounded all through the forest. The little mouse heard it. He recognised the voice of the lion. It was the same one who had spared his life. So he ran to where the lion was. There, tangled in the net of ropes lay the King of the Beasts.

"Greetings, your majesty," said the mouse. "Remember what I said? I know you did not believe me. But see? Here is my chance."

At once the mouse set to work. He nibbled with his sharp little teeth. Working swiftly, he cut through the ropes. Soon the lion was free. He crawled gratefully out of the hunters' snare.

A Write down the words in List A. Next to each write the word or phrase from List B that could replace it in the passage without changing the meaning.

A	B
with a start	refused to take
squealed	trap
amused by	knowing
recognising	laughing at
spared	with a sudden jump
tangled	bite with small bites
nibble	knotted up
snare	cried in a squeaky voice

B Choose the best answer to complete each sentence. Copy the sentences into your books.

1. The lion woke with a start because
   a) he was surprised in his sleep b) he was angry
   c) he was ready for action.
2. The lion clapped his paw on the mouse and roared because he was
   a) sleepy b) angry c) hungry.
3. The little mouse squealed when he begged the lion to let him go because
   a) he had a bad throat b) he was scared
   c) he was calling for help.
4. The lion let the mouse go because
   a) he was a kind lion
   b) the mouse promised to pay him
   c) he was amused by the thought that such a tiny creature could help him.
5. The hunters caught the lion
   a) by shooting him with arrows b) by digging a pit
   c) by trapping him in a net.
6. The mouse knew that the lion was the one who had let him go because
   a) that was the only lion in the forest
   b) he recognised the lion's roar
   c) he saw the hunters trap the lion.

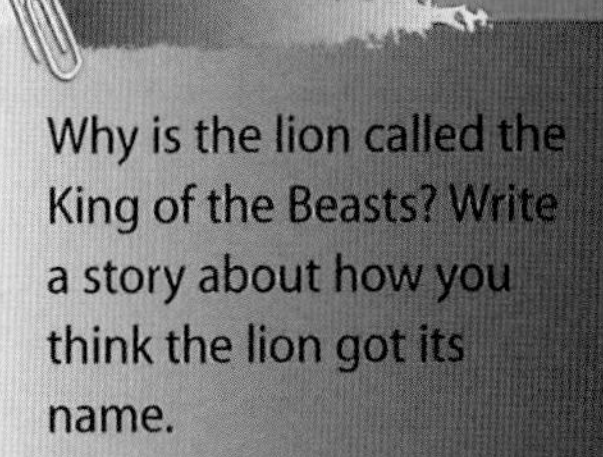

Editing; more dictionary work

A Here is a letter that Fred wrote to Ray to tell him about his holiday. He was in a hurry so he did not edit the letter. Copy the letter, correcting Fred's mistakes. Follow these steps.

1. Make a list of all the words that Fred spelled incorrectly. Put them in alphabetical order, and then use your dictionary to check the spelling.
2. Look for the places where Fred left out capitals. Put these in.
3. There are several places where Fred omitted to use the apostrophe. Find where these are and put the apostrophes in.
4. In some sentences, the verbs do not agree with the subjects. Change the verbs so that they agree with the subjects.
5. Look for the places where he used the wrong tenses. Correct the tenses.
6. Read through the letter more than once to see if you have found all the errors.

B Dear Ray,

I am having a reelly good time at my uncles farm. Its a great place to be in the sumer. There is lots of thing to do. Last week we go to the beach three time. then on sunday my uncle take us to a place in the hills near st. ann where there was all Kinds of birds. There was humminbirds and canaries and sparrow and hawks and woodpickers. I dont have enuff space to tell you all the name and besides I dont Know all of them.

Ill write agayn next week with more news.

Your fren, Fred

Similar words

a courageous sailor
a brave sailor

The words **courageous** and **brave** are similar in meaning.

aged	old
connect	join
select	choose
loiter	linger
slender	slim
cash	money
garments	clothes
pretty	beautiful
plump	fat
tremble	shake

A Learn the similar words in the list on the left. Then write these sentences in your books, replacing each word in bold type with a word that has a similar meaning.

1. The **cash** was taken to the bank.
2. The plumber came to **connect** the pipes.
3. He was a very **pretty** child.
4. Mother bought a **plump** chicken for dinner.
5. You should not **loiter** on the way home.
6. The boys had to **choose** a captain for the team.
7. The dancer had a **slender** figure.
8. An **aged** woman opened the door.
9. The train made the old bridge **tremble**.
10. All **garments** sold in this shop are made of cotton.

B Write short sentences using simpler words that are similar in meaning to these. You learnt some of these words in Book 1. Use your dictionaries if you need to.

1. broad	6. collect	11. wealthy
2. clever	7. difficult	12. weeping
3. finish	8. farewell	13. correct
4. large	9. commence	14. peril
5. repair	10. reply	15. assist

Telling the time

A Look at the number to which the big hand points on each clock. Learn the times shown.

five minutes past

ten minutes past

twenty minutes past

twenty minutes to

five minutes to

ten minutes to

B Each of these clocks shows the time a plane, bus or boat leaves. Copy the sentences and complete them by writing the time of departure for each mode of transport.

1. The boat to Williamsfield leaves at _______

2. The boat to Plymouth leaves at _______

3. The plane to Kingstown leaves at _______

4. The bus to Castries leaves at _______

5. The bus to Toco leaves at _______

6. The plane to Tobago leaves at _______

Forming adjectives by using the suffix –ful

A **suffix** is one or more syllables placed at the **end** of a word to make a new word with a new meaning. We form many adjectives by adding the suffix **–ful** to a noun.

hope + full = hopeful
(full of hope)
joy + full = joyful
(full of joy)

Note that in adding **–full** one **l** is dropped.

- beautiful
- peaceful
- careful
- playful
- harmful
- thankful
- helpful
- truthful
- painful
- useful

A Choose from the list on the left the adjective ending with **–ful** that will fill each gap.

1. a kitten that is full of play — a ______ kitten
2. a town in which there is peace — a ______ town
3. a girl of great beauty — a ______ girl
4. a driver who takes great care — a ______ driver
5. a cut that gives much pain — a ______ cut
6. a book that is of great use — a ______ book
7. a friend who gives help — a ______ friend
8. a person who is full of thanks — a ______ person
9. a boy who speaks the truth — a ______ boy
10. a habit that causes harm — a ______ habit

B Add **–ful** to each of these words. Then choose three of the words you have made and use them in sentences of your own, one word in each sentence.

1. shame 2. delight 3. wonder
4. cheer 5. fear 6. hate

Using adjectives

1. The man walked down the road.
2. The old man walked down the road.

Sentence 2 is better than Sentence 1 because it tells us something about the man. He was old.

3. The old man walked down the dusty road.

Sentence 3 is better than either Sentence 1 or 2 because it also tells us something about the road. It was dusty.

clever	cool
ripe	broken-down
greedy	delicious
bright	fierce
empty	dusty
large	hungry
blue	kind
biggest	angry
juicy	big
rickety	cane

A Copy this passage, filling each space with a suitable adjective from the list on the left.

It was a _______ day. A _______ breeze was blowing. Bunches of _______ mangoes swung on the trees. A _______ boy was passing by. He looked at the _______ mango. He rubbed his _______ stomach. "What a _______ mango," he said. Suddenly a _______ dog rushed out. He snarled at the _______ boy. The boy ran down the _______ road. The _______ dog chased him through a _______ field. He ran into a _______ building and shut the _______ door as quickly as he could. The _______ dog sat outside the door waiting.

B Use each pair of nouns in a sentence with an adjective to describe each noun.

1. sun sky
2. boy lesson
3. rain streets
4. lightening clouds
5. waves boats
6. ship survivors

Writing dates

We can use short forms to write the date.

We write **–st** after some numbers.

1st	first
21st	twenty-first
31st	thirty-first

We write **–nd** after some numbers.

2nd	second
22nd	twenty-second

We write **–rd** after some numbers.

3rd	third
23rd	twenty-third

For all other numbers in the calendar we add **–th**.

4th	fourth
11th	eleventh
17th	seventeenth
25th	twenty-fifth

A Use numbers to write these.

1. fifth
2. first
3. ninth
4. fourth
5. twenty-third
6. tenth
7. sixth
8. twenty-first
9. thirty-first
10. twelfth
11. second
12. third
13. sixteenth
14. seventh
15. twenty-second

B Answer these questions in complete sentences in your books. Use the short forms for months and days.

1. How would you write the twenty-fourth of September in a letter?
2. On which date does New Year's Day come?
3. What is the date today?
4. What is the date of your birthday?
5. How would you write August the twenty-first in your diary?
6. On which date does Christmas Day come?

Poetry: The Moon

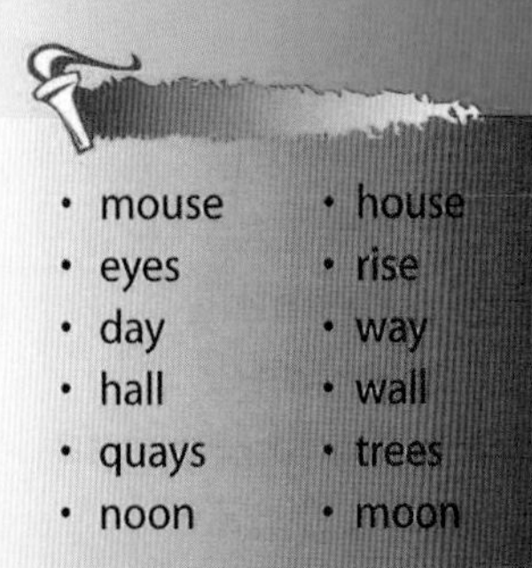

A Copy the poem, filling in the missing words. You will find these rhyming words in the list.

The Moon

The moon has a face like the clock in the hall,
She shines on thieves on the garden _______ ;
On streets and fields and harbour _______ ,
And birdies asleep in the forks of _______ .

The squalling cat and the squeaking mouse,
The howling dog by the door of the _______ ;
The bat that lies in bed at _______ ,
All love to be out by the light of the _______ .

But all of the things that belong to the day,
Cuddle to sleep to be out of her _______ ;
And flowers and children close their _______ ,
Till up in the morning the sun shall _______ .

Read the poem silently. Talk about how to read it with expression. Which lines should you read loudly? Softly? In a normal voice? Should some words (e.g. squeaking) be read in special ways? Read the poem aloud several times.

B In each group below write three other words that rhyme with the word in bold type. The first letters are given to help you.

1. bat	**2.** sand	**3.** tack
r _ _	h _ _ _	r _ _ _
h _ _	b _ _ _	b _ _ _
p _ _	l _ _ _	s _ _ _

Verbs: using ate/has eaten/have eaten

Rule: Add **–ed** to the root verb to form the simple past tense.

Eat is an **irregular** verb. It is irregular because it does **not follow the rule** to add **–ed** to show the past tense. Instead, it changes the form (or shape) of the root verb.

To show the past time of **eat** we use **ate**. The word ate does not need a helping word.

George **ate** his mango.

We can also use **has eaten**, **have eaten** and **had eaten** for past time. The word eaten always needs one of the helping words **has**, **have** or **had**.

George **has eaten** his mango.
George and Max **have eaten** their mangoes.
George **had eaten** his mango.

A Use **ate** or **eaten** to fill each space.

1. I _______ the smallest piece of pie.
2. You have _______ four pieces.
3. My brothers have _______ the biggest slices.
4. Al _______ three in all.
5. I _______ one.
6. Sue has _______ four.
7. All together we had _______ eight.
8. They have not _______ yet.
9. She has _______ , and so have we.
10. We had _______ all but three patties.

B Use **ate** or **eaten** to fill each space.

1. John _______ his supper.
2. His mother said, "John, since you have _______ , you can go out to play."
3. The monkey had _______ all the nuts the children had given him.
4. "Look," Hal said, "he has _______ the nuts and he's climbing the tree."
5. "Oh dear," said Mother Hubbard, when she saw that the children had _______ all the porridge.
6. "I have _______ none," she said, "so I'll have to make some more."
7. When Barb has _______ supper, she may go up to her room.
8. When the rest of you have _______ your supper, please clear the table.

Comprehension: Androcles and the lion

arrested means seized
refused means said "No"

Long ago, there was a shepherd named Androcles. One day, he was roaming through the hot desert. Suddenly he met a lion. At first he was very fearful. Then he saw that the lion had a thorn in its paw. It was in terrible pain. He walked towards it. Gently, he spoke to it. Then he pulled out the thorn. From that time on, Androcles and the lion were great friends.

Some time later some soldiers came. They arrested Androcles. They forced him to travel far across the sea. They dragged him to the great city of Rome. The Emperor of Rome tried to make Androcles give up his Christian faith. Androcles refused. The Emperor made his soldiers throw Androcles into a huge arena. They were going to send in a fierce lion. The lion would tear him apart and eat him.

Androcles saw the lion spring towards him. Then, suddenly, it stopped. It bowed its head. It held out its paw. Androcles knew then who it was. It was his friend from the desert. Hunters had trapped him too. They had brought him from the desert to Rome.

The Emperor was amazed. "You and your lion have been loyal and brave, Androcles," he said. "I shall free you both."

So Androcles and the lion went back across the sea. They were happy to return to their desert home in Africa.

A Find words in the passage that match the meanings below.

1. wandering around
2. dry, bare, sandy place
3. faithful
4. savage, violent
5. astonished, greatly surprised

B Use four adjectives from the story in sentences of your own.

C Read these sentences about the story. Write them in the order in which the events happened.

1. Androcles was arrested by the Roman Emperor because he refused to give up his Christian faith.
2. The lion did not eat Androcles because this was his friend from the desert of Africa.
3. Androcles met a lion in the African desert.
4. Androcles and the lion were set free and they returned to Africa.
5. The lion and Androcles became great friends after he pulled out a thorn from its paw.
6. Androcles was thrown into the arena to be eaten by a lion.

Work in pairs, if your teacher agrees. Imagine the conversation between Androcles and the lion as they get off the boat and stand on the shores of their home country again. Write it in dialogue form.

Opposites: change of word

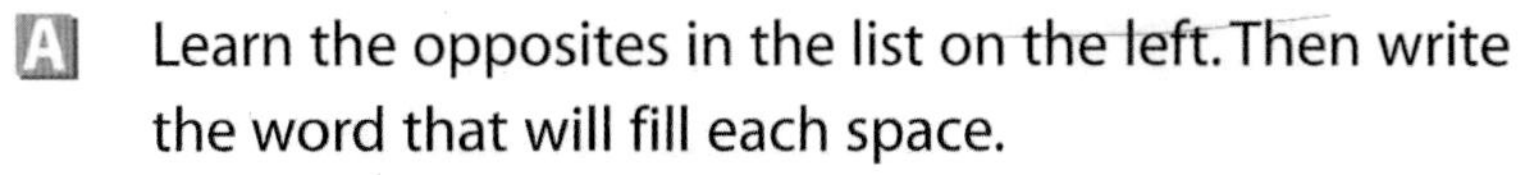

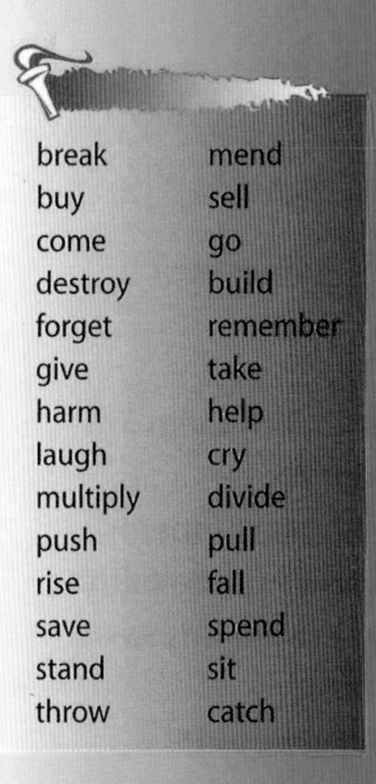

break	mend
buy	sell
come	go
destroy	build
forget	remember
give	take
harm	help
laugh	cry
multiply	divide
push	pull
rise	fall
save	spend
stand	sit
throw	catch

A Learn the opposites in the list on the left. Then write the word that will fill each space.

1. You pull to open the door and _____ to close it.
2. Well, usually I remember that's the way it works, but sometimes I _____ .
3. In life you have to learn to give and _____ .
4. And you also have to learn to _____ and cry.
5. You must try not to _____ but to help.
6. And if you fall, you should _____ right away.
7. And you must not only spend but also _____ .

B Replace the verbs in bold type in the passages with opposites chosen from the list.

1.

On Fridays, the potters (**give**) their wares to market where they (**buy**) them. They sometimes (**remember**) to make sure the pots are steady in the cart. If the carts jolt when the drivers (**stand**) down, the pots can (**mend**). This can also occur if the carts (**rise**) into a hole in the road. Sudden movement can (**build**) many pots.

2.

"How can this training (**come**) anywhere?" the coach said. "First I see Sandra (**push**) Mary's hair. Then I see Mary start to (**laugh**). Why should I (**save**) time with players who don't want to (**harm**) themselves? Serious athletes don't (**multiply**) their time between fighting and playing!" Then she turned to (**catch**) the ball to the captain and walked off field.

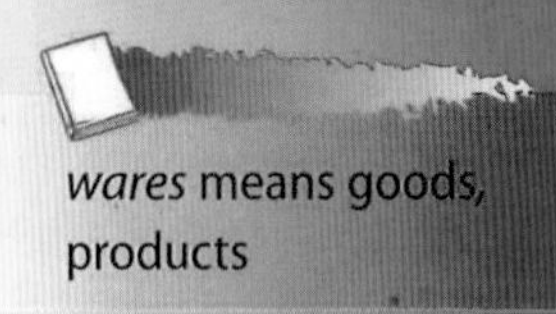

wares means goods, products

Homophones (4)

Homophones are words that have the same sound but they differ in spelling and meaning.

pain He felt no **pain** when he had his tooth out.

pane He put a new **pane** of glass in the window.

road Many cars were parked at the side of the **road**.

rode Ian **rode** to school on his new bicycle.

sail The strong wind tore one **sail** of the ship.

sale All goods were very cheap at the **sale**.

there I left the dish **there** on the table. (in that place)

their The two boys had lost **their** pencils. (belonging to them)

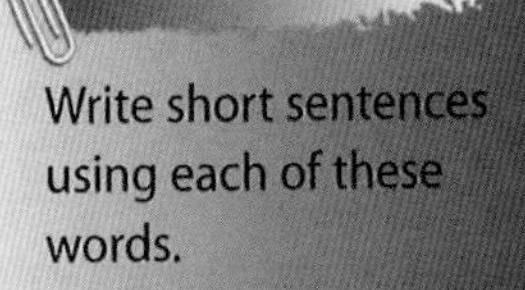

Write short sentences using each of these words.

A Look at the four pairs of words on the left. Learn to spell each word. Learn the meaning of each.

B Choose the correct word from the pair to complete each sentence.

1. The _______ was muddy after the heavy rain. (**road/rode**)
2. Helen bought the carpet at a ______ . (**sail/sale**)
3. Susan had a _______ in her arm. (**pain/pane**)
4. Alan _______ his donkey up the hill. (**road/rode**)
5. We waited _______ for an hour. (**there/their**)
6. The cricket ball broke a _______ in the window. (**pain/pane**)
7. The _______ of the yacht was lowered as it reached the shore. (**sail/sale**)
8. The children found ______ football in the hedge. (**there/their**)

Using gave and given

Give is an **irregular** verb. It is irregular because it does **not follow the rule** to add **–ed** to show the past tense. Instead, it changes the form (or shape) of the root verb.

To show the past time of **give** we use **gave**.

Lydia **gave** Tina a pencil.

We can also use **has given**, **have given** and **had given** for past time. The word given always needs one of the helping words **has**, **have** or **had**.

Lydia **has given** Tina her pencil.
Lydia and Tina **have given** away their pencils.
Lydia **had given** her pencil away.

A Use **gave** or **given** to fill each space.

1. She has _______ it all away.
2. You have _______ nothing.
3. We _______ what we could.
4. I have _______ all my time.
5. You had _______ before.
6. We have _______ far too little.
7. The lion had _______ the mouse his life.
8. The mouse _______ the lion the same gift.
9. The woman _______ the clouds a smack.
10. Stories have _______ children great fun.

B Write the word that fills each space.

1. The teacher _______ each child a birthday present.
2. They _______ her a birthday present too.
3. The teacher had _______ Ann the pencils so she could sharpen them.
4. After she did, Ann _______ out all the pencils.
5. Ann has _______ Carol the last pencil, so she has no pencil for herself.
6. Terry _______ me a big ripe mango.
7. I had _______ him oranges yesterday.
8. Kingsley _______ his parents a kiss before going to bed.
9. He has _______ them a kiss every night since he was a little boy.
10. Mary was happy that she had _______ all her sweets away.
11. She always ate too many and they always _______ her a tummy ache.

Sounds

- patter
- toot
- ringing
- beat
- clatter
- ticking
- singing
- slam

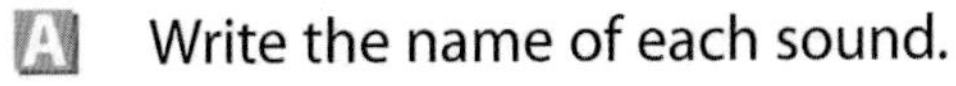

A Write the name of each sound.

1. the ______ of dishes
2. the ______ of a drum
3. the ______ of bells
4. the ______ of a clock
5. the ______ of a door
6. the ______ of a horn
7. the ______ of a kettle
8. the ______ of raindrops

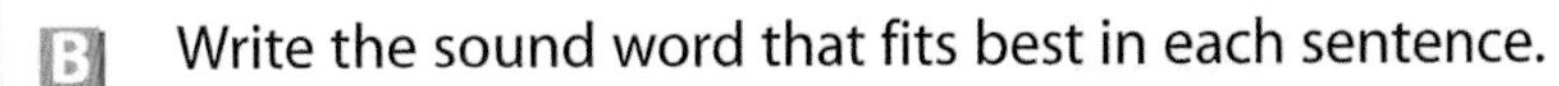

B Write the sound word that fits best in each sentence.

1. The ______ of raindrops on the window awakened the children.
2. We heard the ______ of drums as the soldiers drew near.
3. The room was so quiet that we could hear the ______ of the clock.
4. The ______ of the kettle told us that the water was boiling.
5. From the kitchen came the ______ of dishes.
6. With a ______ of the door Brian left the room.
7. The car went past with a ______ of the horn.
8. Every Sunday the ______ of church bells could be heard in the village.

More compound words

The word **where** can be joined to **any, every, no** and **some.**

any + where = anywhere
every + where = everywhere
no + where = nowhere
some + where = somewhere

The word **body** can be joined to **any, every, no** and **some.**

any + body = anybody
every + body = everybody
no + body = nobody
some + body = somebody

The word **ever** can be joined to **when, where, who, what, how** and **which.**

when + ever = whenever
where + ever = wherever
who + ever = whoever
what + ever = whatever
how + ever = however
which + ever = whichever

A Use one of the compound (or joined) **–where** words to fill each space.

"The hammer must be ______ in the house," Janet said. We looked ______ for it. Although we searched, the hammer was ______ to be seen. We all searched and we could not find it ______ .

B Use one of the compound **–body** words to fill each space.

I don't want to go to that school because I won't know ______ . My Mum and Dad say I'm sure to see ______ that I've met before, but ______ that I know is going to that school. ______ is going to the high school in town.

C Write the **–ever** words which will finish these sentences.

1. He never wears a hat, ______ cold the weather is.
2. People must buy food, ______ it costs.
3. ______ took the money must give it back.
4. You can visit us ______ you like.
5. ______ you hide, we will find you.
6. ______ road you take, it will lead to the centre of the town.

Poetry: Rain Clouds

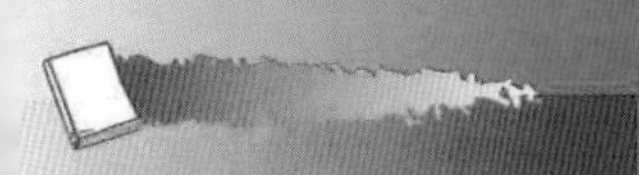

caravan means a group of merchants travelling together with goods to sell, often through the desert on camels

Rain Clouds

Along a road
Not built by man
There winds a silent
Caravan
Of camel-clouds
Whose humped gray backs
Are weighted down
With heavy packs
Of long-awaited,
Precious rain
To make the old earth
Young again,
And dress her shabby
Fields and hills
In green grass silk
With wild-flower frills.

Elizabeth-Ellen Long

A Read the poem silently, once or twice, and then read it aloud together, as many times as you wish.

B Answer these questions in your books.

1. What is the caravan made of? Why is the road *not made by man*?
2. What are the goods that are being carried in the *heavy packs*?
3. Why are the fields and hills *shabby*?
4. How will the *old earth* become young again?
5. The old earth is being described as a person. Is it a man or a woman?

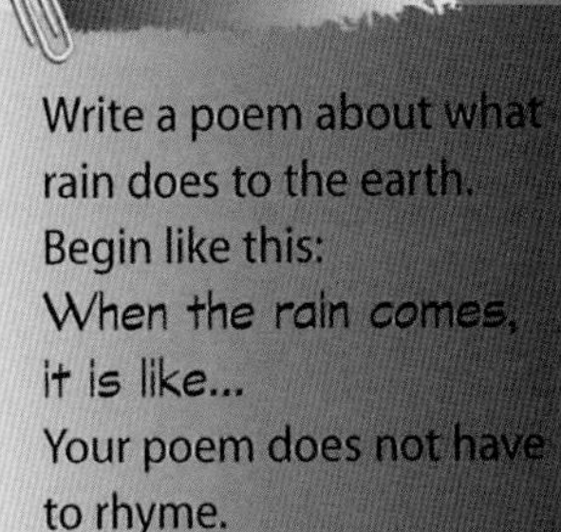

Write a poem about what rain does to the earth. Begin like this:
When the rain comes, it is like...
Your poem does not have to rhyme.

Comprehension: Water

Water covers most of the earth's surface. Much of it is in rivers, lakes, seas and oceans. Where does it come from? The answer is simple. It was always here. Every drop of water that was present when the earth began is still here. It may be in liquid form. It may be in gas or solid form. But it exists.

We can see the water in rivers, lakes, seas and oceans. But there is plenty of water where we can't see it. And this water is very crucial. When rain falls and hits the ground, it doesn't all go to the same place. The sun dries up some. Plants absorb some. Some runs off the land into streams and rivers. Some sinks into the ground and stays there to keep the soil wet. But some trickles further down. It keeps going until it meets the water that is already deep in the earth. This deep-down water fills all the spaces and cracks between rocks, stones and grains of soil. We call this water, ground water. The top part of ground water is called the water table.

Why is ground water important? Because it is the water in nature's dam. We dig wells until they reach ground water. Ground water supplies the water in springs. It forms lakes, ponds, swamps and marshes. It is part of rivers that run through underground passageways in the earth. It is in waterfalls that splash down the sides of underground caves. It is in pools in deep caves. The healing waters in mineral springs also come from ground water.

A Find these words in the passage. Then choose meaning that matches the way the word is used.

1. Surface means
   a) cover
   b) outer part
   c) flatness.
2. Exists means
   a) is present
   b) is alive
   c) can be seen.
3. Crucial means
   a) very expensive
   b) important
   c) hard to reach.
4. Absorb means
   a) understand
   b) soak up
   c) attract.
5. Healing means
   a) curing
   b) warming
   c) healthy.

B

1. Where is much of the water on the earth's surface to be found?
2. Where does all the water come from?
3. How many forms can water take?
4. What is ground water?
5. What is the water table?
6. Why is ground water so important?

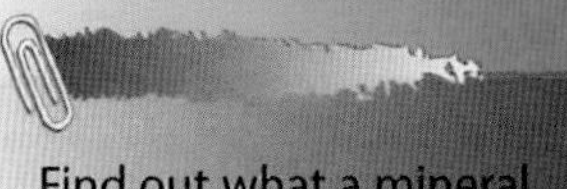

Find out what a mineral spring is. Where do the healing powers in the water of mineral springs come from?

C Either write some sentences to explain what is meant by *nature's dam* or write some sentences that tell all the different things that happen to rain when it falls on the land.

More opposites

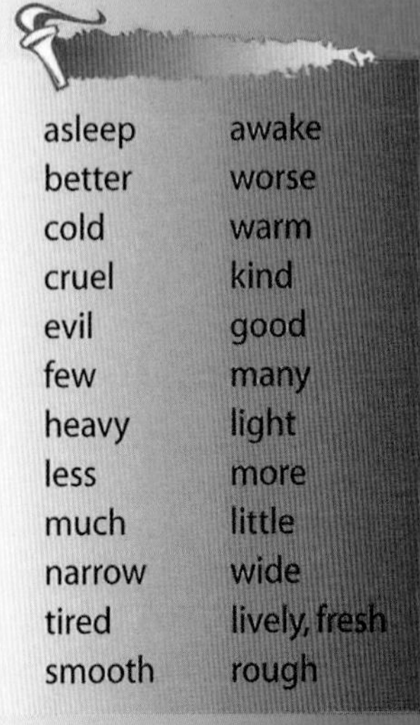

A Copy the sentences. Choose the opposite of the word in bold type and use it to fill the space.

1. The little boy had a kind master. (**cruel**)
2. He knew that he and his master were in ____ danger. (**little**)
3. An ____ prince was after them. (**good**)
4. So it would be ____ for them to be far away in another country. (**worse**)
5. The boy knew that his master was ____ . (**lively**)
6. In fact, his master was fast ____ . (**awake**)
7. "Wake up, master," the boy said. "We can't waste any ____ time." (**less**)
8. As they set off, a ____ breeze blew. (**cold**)
9. There was ____ rain falling. (**light**)
10. The road was very ____ . (**wide**)
11. It was also very ____ . (**smooth**)
12. But it was a good way to go for ____ people travelled there. (**many**)

B Write the word that will fill each space.

1. Strong winds made the sea very ____ .
2. The red box is ____ but the blue one is light.
3. The men wanted more pay and ____ work.
4. She could tell by his ____ smile that he was ready to help.
5. Mother was ____ after a long hard day at work.
6. At seven o'clock Pat was wide awake, but Judith was still ____ .

Words with more than one meaning (2)

Some words have more than one meaning.

We went to visit an old silver **mine** in the mountains.
The red towel is **mine** but the blue one belongs to Sally.

- blind
- felt
- foot
- long
- mean
- ring
- rock
- suit
- top
- trunk

A Use the words in the list to fill these spaces. The same word must be used for each pair of sentences.

1. The dress is too ____ so I must shorten it.
   I often ____ for a holiday in the country.
2. The miser was too ____ to buy food for himself.
   Some words ____ much the same thing as other words.
3. I think this dress will ____ you.
   Henry wore a navy blue ____ to the wedding.
4. The teddy bear was made of ____ .
   Carol ____ ill, so she went to bed early.
5. A ____ person cannot see.
   She pulled the ____ down over the window.
6. Errol put the suitcases in the ____ of the car.
   The elephant took the bun with his long ____ .
7. There was a river at the ____ of the mountain.
   He was lame because he had hurt his ____ .
8. Please ____ the doorbell.
   Emma wore a ____ on every finger.
9. On the beach was a huge ____ .
   Jane tried to ____ the baby to sleep.
10. Humpty Dumpty was sitting on ____ of the wall.
    The red ____ was spinning round and round.

Write six sentences using any three of the words in the list. You must use them with both meanings.

Joining sentences using and, because, so and but

You know how to join sentences with **and**. The word **because** can also be used to join two sentences.

- The dog bit John.
- He was teasing it.

The dog bit John because he was teasing it.

A Use **because** to join these sentences.

1. Roy was very happy.
   There was a holiday.
2. He did not drink his tea.
   It was cold.
3. Shanti went to bed early.
   She had a sore throat.
4. We closed the windows.
   It started raining.
5. She passed the test.
   She studied very hard.

B Write the missing word **and**, **so**, **but** or **because** in each sentence.

1. Barbara made lots of cookies _______ she gave some away.
2. The bus was crowded _______ of the cricket match.
3. Al went fishing _______ he didn't catch anything.
4. The wind became stronger _______ the rain began to fall heavily.
5. Jean dropped the cup _______ it did not break.
6. We went to church early _______ we were going to the beach.
7. The boys went outside _______ spent the morning playing football.
8. He drove slowly through the puddles _____ he wouldn't splash anyone.

Things that are alike

When something is very light in weight we say it is **as light as a feather**. This is because a feather is very, very light.

Learn the comparisons in the list below.
- as black as pitch
- as blind as a bat
- as brown as a berry
- as easy as ABC
- as green as grass
- as hard as nails
- as hot as fire
- as soft as putty
- as stiff as a board
- as weak as a kitten

These comparisons may work in other ways. Some people say "as hard as a rock". Talk about other ways of making these comparisons.

A Talk about the comparisons on the left. Do you think they are good ones? Can you think of better ones?

B Write the missing words.

1. as weak as a ______
2. as easy as ______
3. as green as ______
4. as stiff as a ______
5. as blind as a ______
6. as black as ______
7. as hard as ______
8. as soft as ______

C Write the missing words.

1. as ______ as fire
2. as ______ as nails
3. as ______ as a board
4. as ______ as pitch
5. as ______ as grass
6. as ______ as a kitten
7. as ______ as a bat
8. as ______ as a berry

D Write the missing words.

1. John felt as weak as a ______ after his illness.
2. The soldier standing at attention was as _____ as a board.
3. He returned from the seaside as ______ as a berry.
4. The bed he slept on was as hard as ______ .
5. Andrew found the sum as ______ as ABC.
6. The sand on the beach was as hot as ______ .
7. The kitten had fur as black as ______ .
8. Without his glasses, he was as ______ as a bat.

Sentences

A Write the beginning of each sentence. Then choose the ending that will match it.

	Beginning	**Ending**
1.	If you want any help	Dan was hot and tired.
2.	It was raining heavily	in a dozen.
3.	As Ed had a fever	please let me know.
4.	After cutting the grass	and went off to school.
5.	The camel is often called	because there had been no rain.
6.	The load carried by a ship	because he had eaten too much.
7.	Paul picked up his bag	he did not go to school.
8.	The greedy boy was ill	is called a cargo.
9.	Water was scarce	so Allan put on his raincoat.
10.	There are twelve things	the Ship of the Desert.

B Add endings to these sentences.

1. Roger burst into tears…
2. Just as I left the house…
3. Every Christmas Eve…
4. While the cook was baking cakes…
5. During the hurricane…

C Begin each sentence in your own way.

1. …a very long way from home.
2. … and we were soaking wet.
3. …because he felt so tired.
4. …so we could not travel by car.
5. …but it would not move.

Sophia Solomon's Advice Column

A *columnist* is someone who writes a regular column for a newspaper or magazine.
A *reporter* writes news.
A *feature writer* writes special, usually long, articles about one particular subject.

Dear Ms. Solomon,
I am in Grade four. I get three hours of homework every day. I think this is too much. Also, I have chores. I have no time to play.
Please help me,
Desperate Dan

Dear Sophia Solomon,
I board with a family. I like them, except for the little boy. He is five. He is mean. He bites and pinches, really hard. He also steals my things. He does these things when no one is around. His parents and sisters really love him. How can I get them to see that he is a monster child?
Yours truly,
Pinched and Bitten Mary

Dear Ms. Solomon,
My brother calls me Runt. It makes me furious. My father speaks to him but he does it anyway. Please help me to make him stop.
Furious

Make up a letter to Ms. Solomon. Ask her advice on something that is bothering you. Be sure to give her the facts she needs if she is to help you.

A Talk about how you would answer these letters. Does it make a difference that Ms. Solomon cannot tell whether Furious is a boy or a girl? Explain why or why not.

B Pretend you are Sophia Solomon and reply to these letters, suggesting solutions to the children's problems.

That night, not long after Marcus had left, everything was still. The lights were out. The bedroom windows were open. Everyone was fast asleep, or almost everyone. Grandma was the one person who was awake. She was thinking about Marcus, poor Marcus who was all alone in his makeshift house outside.

Grandma was wondering about Marcus's comfort. She knew he had no pillow or mattress to lie on. She knew he had no blanket to cover him, and no proper bed. She also knew that he wanted none of these things. He lived a hard life with few everyday comforts. She realized that the night was hot and there wasn't the slightest chance of rain. However, she felt that a pillow for Marcus's head was essential. So she got up, without disturbing Grandpa, and took the pillowcase from one of her pillows. She tucked the pillow under her arm and crept cautiously into the dining room. There she began searching very quietly for a clean flour bag that she had placed at the back of the sideboard. She found it, pushed the pillow down into it and then patted it till it was smooth all over.

Outside she saw Marcus kneeling a little way from his house and talking to himself. Grandma hesitated. Seeing him made her think of her own son. She listened carefully and heard some of the words Marcus was saying. He was praying. She waited, clutching the pillow closely. She followed Marcus's prayer, word after word, until he came to the end. He prayed with firm belief. She felt that deep down he must be a very special kind of young man.

Marcus looked round and saw her watching him. "Nice night, lady," he said softly.

"Yes," Grandma replied.

"Got something for me?" Marcus asked.

"Yes, a pillow. Do you want one?"

"Thank you." He stood and waited.

She went up to him and handed him the pillow.

Adapted from *Earthquake* by Andrew Salkey

A Choose the best meaning for these words as they are used in the passage. Write the words and their correct meanings in your books.

1. Makeshift means
   a) put-together b) shifty c) falling down.
2. Wondering means
   a) moving about b) believing c) considering.
3. Essential means
   a) unimportant b) necessary c) nice.
4. Cautiously means
   a) fearfully b) carefully c) on tiptoe.
5. Hesitated means
   a) paused b) looked around c) moved along.
6. Clutching means
   a) touching b) holding tightly c) reaching for.

B Choose the best answer and copy each completed sentence into your books.

1. Marcus's house was
   a) large and well-built b) small and solid c) simple and rough.
2. Marcus lived
   a) a hard life b) a comfortable life c) a sad life.
3. Grandma felt that a pillow for Marcus was
   a) unnecessary b) necessary c) better than he deserved.
4. Grandma listened to Marcus's prayer
   a) carelessly b) not at all c) very closely.
5. You can tell from this passage that Grandma is
   a) kind and thoughtful b) stuck-up and selfish c) silly and sappy.
6. You can tell from the passage that Marcus is
   a) a selfish, tough person b) a clever liar c) a gentle, polite man.

C Match the beginnings and endings of these sentences. Put in the correct punctuation.

when marcus left that night	marcus down on his knees
everyone else was asleep	one of her own pillows
she was thinking about poor marcus	but grandma was awake
the night was hot and there	her son in Montego Bay
grandma took the pillowcase from	listened to every word
when she went outside she saw	everything was quiet
he made her think of	in his roughly built house
he was saying his prayers and she	was no chance of rain

D Put the sentences below into the correct order.

1. She went to the dining room and looked for a clean flour bag to cover the pillow.
2. She stopped and listened when she heard Marcus praying.
3. Grandma was worried about whether Marcus was comfortable.
4. She took the pillow outside to give to Marcus.
5. She thought that he truly believed and was sure he was a special young man.
6. She took a pillowcase off of one of her pillows.

E Write out the subject of the verb in these sentences.

1. Grandpa opened the windows.
2. The heat was getting worse.
3. Grandma clutched the pillow.
4. Her son lived in Montego Bay.
5. Marcus was kneeling on the ground.

F Change the subject and the verb in each of these sentences to the plural.

1. The window bangs in the wind.
2. The light goes out suddenly.
3. The night is very hot.
4. The old woman gets up quietly.
5. The man prays on his knees.

G Find words in the passage similar in meaning to these verbs.

- departed
- desired
- started
- put
- rose

H Find words in the passage similar in meaning to these adjectives.

- difficult
- pleasant
- quietly
- short
- spotless

I Find words in the passage that sound the same as these words.

- know
- flower
- new
- nun
- sun

J Write out the following shortened forms without using the apostrophe.

1. Couldn't
2. Grandma's son
3. It's
4. They're
5. There's
6. How's

K Find words in the passage that rhyme with these words.

- book
- dance
- door
- farm
- head
- hill
- mouse
- peep
- sack
- sake

L Use the words below in sentences. They must have meanings that are different from those in the passage.

- fast
- felt
- kind
- left
- lie

M Find and write out five adverbs ending with **–ly** in the passage. Use two of them in sentences.

N There are three compound words in the passage that begin with **every**. Find the sentences in which they are used. Copy them in your books.

O Find five verbs in the passage that show past time by changing their shape (or form). Write out the sentences with these verbs.

P Use one of these prefixes (**dis–**, **mis–**, **re–**, **un–**) with each of the words below to make a new word. Use the new words in sentences.

- belief
- clean
- cover
- took

Q Find compound words in the passage that mean:

- room for a bed
- case for a pillow
- side that is out
- board at the side

R Join these pairs of sentences using **and**, **but**, **because** or **so**.

1. Almost everyone was asleep.
   Grandma was awake.
2. The night was hot.
   The night was still.
3. Marcus was talking to himself.
   Grandma hesitated.
4. He was used to having no proper bed.
   He had lived a very hard life.

S Put each list of words in alphabetical order.

1.	2.	3.
window	outside	clutching
night	open	closely
essential	over	clever
cover	one	climb
rain	own	class

Chart matching this edition against the previous edition of Caribbean Junior English

To the Teacher: Many of the pages in this new edition of *Caribbean Junior English* have the same content as in the previous edition. Some of the page numbers, however, have changed and 29 pages have been added. The following chart will help you to use both editions simultaneously in class.

Page number in this edition	Page number in previous edition	This edition	Previous edition
1	1	Nouns	Nouns: naming words
2	2	Verbs	Verbs: doing words
3	3	Vowels	Vowels
4	7	Adjectives	Adjectives: describing words
5	25	Plurals	Plurals
6	60	Comprehension: The fox and the goat	The fox and the goat
7 **new**		Verbs: forming the simple past tense	
8	6	Verbs: adding –ed to the root verb to form the simple past tense	Verbs: adding –ed and –ing
9	10	Questions	Questions
10/11	11	The weather	The weather
12/13	4/5	Comprehension: The origin of the lamps	The origin of the lamps
14 **new**		Verbs: adding –ing to form the present continuous tense	
15	14	Rhymes	Rhymes
16/17 **new**		Verbs: the present continuous	
18	24 and 39	Dictionary work	Alphabetical order
19	15	Verbs: using is/are, was/were	Using the right word
20/21	36/37	Comprehension: Pitch	Where asphalt comes from
22	19	Using capital letters	Using capital letters
23	18	Words with more than one meaning (1)	Words with more than one meaning
24	8	Developing dialogue	Telephone conversations
25	23	Homophones (1)	Here and hear/There and their
26/27	26/27	Comprehension: Anansi and Snake	Anansi and Snake
28	35	Full stops, commas	Full stops/Commas
29	22	Forming nouns	Forming nouns

This edition	Previous edition	This edition	Previous edition
30	30	Verbs: doubling consonants before adding –ed and –ing	Verbs: adding –ed and –ing
31	33	Verbs: adding –es and –ed	Verbs: adding –es and –ed
32	15	Verbs: did/has done/have done; went/ has gone/have gone	Using the right word
33 **new**		More irregular past tenses	
34/35	46/47	Comprehension: Homeless boys	Homeless boys
36	32	Adjectives: formed by adding –y to nouns	Adjectives: describing words
37 **new**		Subject and verb	
38	31	Joining sentences using so	Joining sentences using so
39	34	Homophones (2)	Same sound – different meaning
40	38	Similar words	Similar words
41	40	Using the apostrophe to show ownership	Showing ownership
42/43 **new**		Comprehension: The conch shell	
44	41	Short forms	Short forms
45	43	Animal noises	Noises of animals
46/47 **new**		Sorting out the story	
48/49	50	Verbs: subjects and verbs agree (1)	Verbs
50	51	Writing letters	Writing letters
51 **new**		Short forms: using the apostrophe	
52/53	54/55	Comprehension: Roland and the turtle	Roland and the turtle
54/55 **new**		Pronouns	
56	52	Opposites: using the prefix -un	Opposites using un
57	53	Collections	Collections
58	56	Occupations	People who work
59	59	Opposites: adjectives	Opposites: change of word
60/61	88/89	Comprehension: Pimento Walk	Pimento Walk
62	58	Animals	Animals
63	62	Groups or categories	Group names
64/65 **new**		Verbs: subject and verb agree (2)	
66	65	The months of the year	The months of the year
67	61	Adverbs	Adverbs
68	78	Using quotation or speech marks	When people speak
69	15	Using as and has	Using the right word
70/71	66/67	Comprehension: How the Pelican got its beak	How the Pelican got its beak
72/73	63	Verbs: more verbs that change to show past time	Verbs: past time
74 **new**		Poetry: Catch a Little Rhyme	
75	72/73	Abbreviated or short forms	Short forms/The long and the short/ Initials

This edition	Previous edition	This edition	Previous edition
76/77 **new**		Building a story	
78/79	45	Writing book reviews	Enjoy a good book!
80	77	Using took and taken	Using took and taken
81	15	Using see, saw and seen	Using the right word
82	64	Homophones (3)	Same sound – different meaning
83	71	Compound words	Compound words
84/85 **new**		How to make a model of a pig	
86	69	Writing instructions	Write the instructions
87	72	Short forms	Short forms
88	80/81	Comprehension: The lion and the mouse	The lion and the mouse
90 **new**		Editing; more dictionary work	
91	79	Similar words	Similar words
92	86	Telling the time	Telling the time
93	83	Forming adjectives by using the suffix –ful	Forming adjectives
94	94	Using adjectives	Using adjectives
95	70	Writing dates	Writing dates
96	92	Poetry: The moon	Rhymes
97	91	Verbs: using ate/has eaten/have eaten	Using ate and eaten
98/99	96/97	Comprehension: Androcles and the lion	Androcles and the lion
100	95	Opposites: change of word	Opposites: change of word
101	98	Homophones (4)	Same sound – different meaning
102	102	Using gave and given	Using gave and given
103	108	Sounds	Sounds
104 **new**		More compound words	
105 **new**		Poetry: Rain Clouds	
106/107 **new**		Comprehension: Water	
108 **new**			More opposites
109	101	Words with more than one meaning (2)	Words with more than one meaning
110	100	Joining sentences using and, because, so, and but	Joining sentences using because
111	103	Things that are alike	Things that are alike
112	93	Sentences	Sentences
113	48/49	Sophia Solomon's Advice Column	Katie's Advice Column
114-118 **new**		Looking back	

Index